Bolos, Bandits, and Bamboo Schools

Michael Dowling's letters from the Philippines during President McKinley's war with Aguinaldo

His plan to transform the schools of Manila and his bizarre interview with the "Sultan of Sulu"

Compiled and edited
by Barry Prichard

Copyright 2009 by Barry Prichard (Grandson) and 1943 by Henrietta "Hattie" Bordewich and the Dowling family.

May not be reproduced or transmitted in any form or by any means, electronic or mechanical, including photocopy, recording or any information storage and retrieval system without permission in writing except for a reviewer who wishes to quote brief passages in connection with a review written for inclusion in a magazine, newspaper or broadcast. All rights reserved. No use without prior permission in writing.

Published by Richards Publishing Co., PO Box 159, Gonvick, MN 56644.
Phone 218-487-5225 * 444-9258 * Fax 218-487-5251
E-mail: richards@gvtel.com

Cover design and map by Jessica Wike

Photographs restored and enhanced by Picture This, Bemidji, MN

Publisher's Cataloging in Publication

BOLOS, BANDITS AND BAMBOO SCHOOLS: Michael Dowling's letters from the Philippines during President McKinley's war with Aguinaldo and his bizarre interview with the "Sultan of Sulu".

Compiled and edited by Barry Prichard

1. Philippines – History – Philippine American War 1899-1902
2. United States – History – President William McKinley
3. Minnesota – History – Michael J. Dowling
4. Philippines – History – The Sultan of Sulu

Library of Congress Control Number: 2009913581
ISBN 978-0-9759180-2-9
First Edition December 2009
Printed in the United States of America

Also About Michael J. Dowling

"**We Blazed the Trail**" by Dorothy Dowling Prichard as told to her son Barry Prichard.

This is the true story of Michael Dowling's motoring trip from Minneapolis to Yellowstone as remembered by his daughter Dorothy. They were the first ones to "Blaze the Trail" by motor car in 1913, before there were roads, bridges or highways!

"I highly recommend this book to all car enthusiasts and history buffs; a book that should be in all area school libraries."

-Francis J. Kalvoda

Available from Richards

Acknowledgements

This book was inspired by my grandmother, Jennie (Bordewich) Dowling. In fact, she predicted I would write it and almost scared me into it. It was a prediction I never forgot, because I was just seven years old and that was the first time she ever allowed me to hold her "beheading sword" brought home from the Philippines by Michael Dowling. That was also the day she told how he pulled his leg on the Sultan of Sulu. But, she never told me the rest of the story. And, that's what this book is about.

Thanks to my great-aunt, Henrietta "Hattie" Bordewich, for copyrighting and preserving Michael Dowling's papers and to my mother, Dorothy (Dowling) Prichard for keeping copies of his letters and recalling his stories. To my aunt Kathleen Dowling who urged me to "for heavens sakes, sit down and write it." To my brother, Michael Prichard, who saved the photographs and helped locate information. To all the aunts, uncles, cousins and various family members who filled in so many bits and pieces of the story.

Heartfelt appreciation to my wife, Joan, and my son, Tim, and daughter Krys, for their patience and support. Thanks as well to Robert A. Fulton, Beverly N. Hermes, William and Madeline Sutherland, Suzanne M. Hilgert, Corrine and Dick Richards, Sue Eck and all of the editors, librarians, historians and veterans of the Philippines who offered assistance. Thanks to all of you for your help and encouragement!

Lastly, thanks to my dog "Mitzi" who walked over a thousand miles with me while I tried to figure out what Michael Dowling was up to in those far-away islands and what his mission was really about.

At the tail-end of it all, I'm still in doubt!

VERY SPECIAL THANKS!

To Joseph N. Rubin for inviting me to the dress rehearsal and opening night performance of "The Sultan of Sulu" revival presented by the Canton Comic Opera Co. on July 16-18-19, 2009.

It was a rare privilege, indeed, to witness the first performance of this historic operetta in 78 years. Inspiration for the original musical came from my grandfather, Michael J. Dowling, who happened to meet George Ade, the playwright. He told Ade about the Sultan's outlandish entourage and way of life and suggested the idea for an "opera bouffe." I believe I recognized a little of my grandfather in the character of Wakeful M. Jones, insurance agent and salesman.

George Ade's light opera creation turned out to be an hilarious musical satire about President McKinley's policy of "Benevolent Assimilation" and American attempts to bring modern civilization to the Sultan and his Muslim followers in the Philippines. But, much of the comic plot and dialogue could just as well be about happenings today.

"The Sultan of Sulu" was first performed in Chicago in 1902. It opened in New York at Wallack's Theatre on December 29, 1902 for a long run of 192 performances. It was last presented by the San Antonio Civic Opera Company in 1931.

Thanks again to Joseph N. Rubin and to all of the talented singers, musicians and folks backstage for a most wonderful performance in 2009.

BARRY PRICHARD is a Captain U.S. Navy Reserve (Retired) who lives by a lake in northern Minnesota.

Table of Contents

Acknowledgements .... Page v

Special Thanks .... Page vi

Map of Philippine Islands .... Page x

Preface .... Page xi

PART I   Dowling's Journey in a Coconut Shell .... Page 3

            Historic Photographs .... Page 25

PART II Dowling's MINNEAPOLIS JOURNAL Articles

           1. ***M.J. Dowling's Trip to Manila*** – First .... Page 45
              Impressions of the Bay and City
              (March 23, 1900/Published May 5, 1900)

           2. ***What They Do in Manila*** – Filipino .... Page 51
              Industries and Life
              (March 28, 1900/Published May 19)

             3. ***Many Chances in Manila*** – How Fortunes .... Page 55
                May be Made
                (March 31, 1900/Published May 26)

             4. ***Manufacturing in Manila*** – Small Factories .... Page 58
                and Their Products
                (April 2, 1900/Published June 2)

             5. ***Iloilo*** – the Canteen, Church at Molo – .... Page 61
                Work of the Sisters
                (April 13, 1900/Published July 6)

             6. ***Cebu*** – Public Education, Filth of Houses, ... Page 68
                Hostility to Americans and Sentiment for Bryan
                (April 17, 1900/Published July 14)

7. **Mindanao** – Visit to Zamboanga, Troops Fat .... Page 76
and Happy, Earthquakes, Soil and Climate
(April 21, 1900/Published July 21)

8. **Dowling Pulls His Leg on the Sultan** – The Harem, .. Page 83
City of Sulu, Weapons, the Sultan Kicks on Pay
(April 23, 1900/Published August 11)

9. **Bongao** – The Rich Pearling Business, Murder of .... Page 92
Four Soldiers and Revenge Taken, Dr. deMey
(April 25, 1900/Published August 25)

10. **Life of Dr. Jose Rizal** – Story of Filipino .... Page 101
Patriot – His Murder by Spaniards
(May 1, 1900/Published September 29)

PART III The Dowling Report (2 Sections)

1. Education in the Philippines .... Page 108
Official Report to the Secretary of War dated
Renville, Minn. July 13th, 1900

2. Confidential Report to the Secretary of War .... Page 122
Education in the Philippines dated Renville,
Minnesota. July 13th, 1900

APPENDIX The Life Story of Michael J. Dowling by the one .... Page 127
who knew him best. Mrs. M.J. (Jennie Bordewich)
Dowling. How he survived that terrible Minnesota
blizzard and how he served his nation and brought
new hope to thousands of disabled men and
women everywhere.

BIBLIOGRAPHY .... Page 135

"I am most anxious for liberties for our country, but I place as a prior condition the education of the people so that our country may have individuality of its own and make itself worthy of liberties."

DR. JOSE' RIZAL,
Philippine Hero and Martyr

"If we do not prepare children to become good citizens- if we do not develop their capacities... then our republic must go down to destruction as others have gone before it."

HORACE MANN,
Father of the American Public School system.

"Human history becomes more and more a race between education and catastrophe."

H.G. WELLES,
written historian

The Philippines

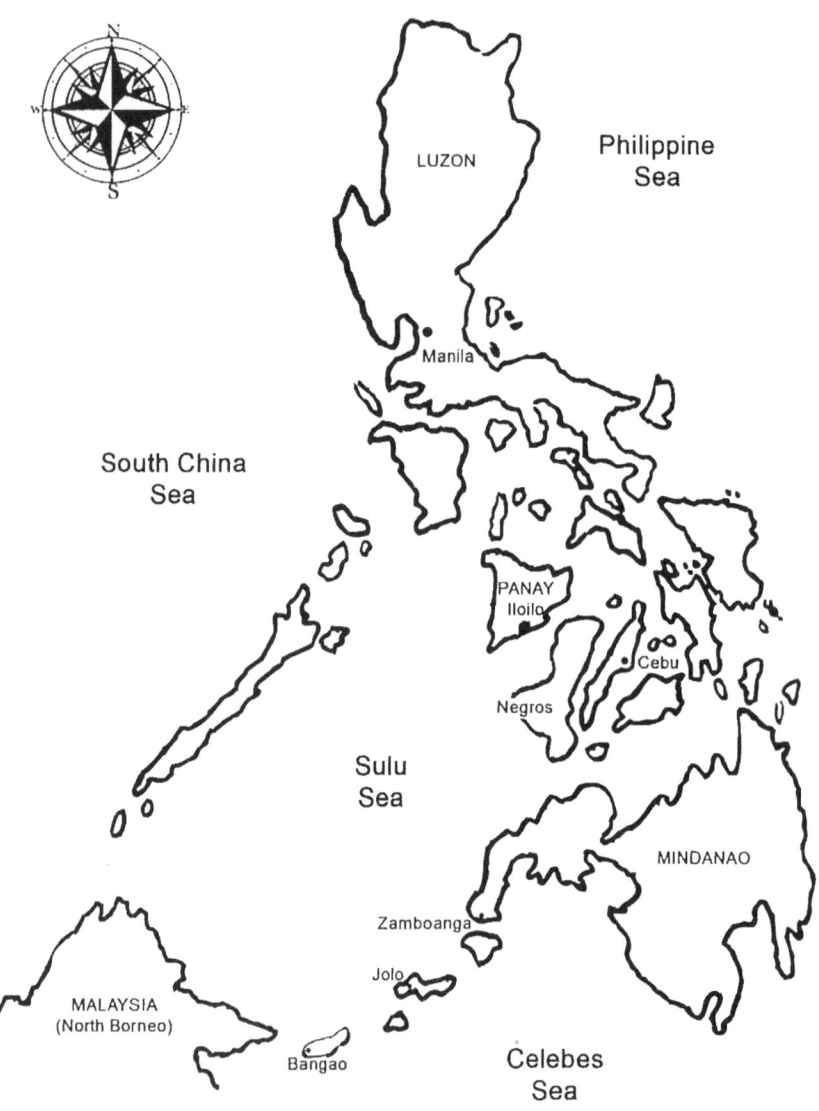

PREFACE

When I started this book, I thought it might be partly about bringing modern education to the Philippines in the aftermath of war, but mostly a humorous tale about my grandfather, Michael J. Dowling, and how he "pulled his leg" on the Sultan of Sulu and inspired the creation of a comic opera. However, I soon realized there was a lot more to the story. And, that much of it was disturbingly relevant to current events!

My grandfather, Michael J. (Jack) Dowling, was an incredible human being. As a boy of 14, he became lost and frozen and almost died in the great Minnesota blizzard of December 1880. Doctors had to amputate both of his feet, amputate one hand and remove all of the fingers from his other hand. "Thank God I'm not a cripple!" he often declared.

Young Jack had been a kid-cowboy, self supporting and on his own from the age of 12. He refused to accept welfare or be placed in foster care for life. Instead, he bargained with the county commissioners to buy him a set of artificial limbs and give him just 2-terms at Carleton College in Northfield, Minnesota. In return, he pledged to never ask for another cent of government aid. True to his word, he went on to become an inspiring teacher and superintendent of schools, a successful insurance agent, an often quoted newspaper editor, a respected banker, the national secretary of the Republican league, a loving husband and father and more!

Then, in 1900, the McKinley administration sent Jack Dowling out to the Philippine Islands by himself, like a single scout ahead of the second Philippine Commission led by Judge W. H. Taft. Dowling had been an important fund-raiser and supporter of President McKinley's nomination and Judge Taft was in line to take over from the Army and become the civil governor of the islands.

Why M.J. Dowling? Why the "wooden Man?" With three artificial limbs, my grandfather would seem a most unlikely person to send across the Pacific Ocean, 8,000 miles around the world, into a dangerous war zone on a one-man, government mission. Officially, he was appointed to visit schools established by the Army and make recommendations about the anticipated change-over from military to civil supervision. But, what was all that other "stuff" that Secretary of War Elihu Root wanted to know? Why was it so SECRET and what did Dowling find to tell him?

Dowling publicly denied the purpose of his trip was to gather information for the U.S. Government. But, his personal letters home say otherwise and suggest there was more to his mission than met the eye. He arrived in Manila on March 14, 1900 and, when not visiting schools, wrote a series of ten articles for the MINNEAPOLIS JOURNAL, covering life in the islands from top to bottom and telling Americans about our war with Aguinaldo. The on-going insurgency had already cost the lives of 1,525 American soldiers killed, an average of 74 deaths a month.

Part I of this book is simply an overview in which I have tried to tell the story of my grandfather's travels "in a coconut shell," put things into historic context, include some photographs and fill in the blanks according to my best understanding.

Part II is a compilation of the ten MINNEAPOLIS JOURNAL articles which my grandfather wrote from the Philippines between March 23 and May 1, 1900. They tell the bizarre story of how he "pulled his leg" on the Sultan of Sulu and about life in Manila, Iloilo, Cebu, Zamboanga, Jolo and Bangao. His final article was a warm and moving interview with the 73-year old mother of Dr. Jose Rizal, the martyred patriot and Philippine national hero.

Part III consists of his official report on Education in the Philippines dated Renville, Minnesota July 13, 1900. The report was submitted to the Secretary of War in two parts, with the second part marked CONFIDENTIAL.

The Appendix is the life story of Michael J. Dowling as told by the one who knew him best, my grandmother, Jennie L. (Bordewich) Dowling. It is a truly inspiring story of courage and determination. How he survived that terrible Minnesota blizzard and how he served his nation and brought new hope to thousands of disabled men and women everywhere.

Mistakes or omissions of research and editing are mine alone. Readers will have to decide for themselves what it was really about?

-Barry Prichard

PART ONE

Dowling's Journey in a Coconut Shell

★ With historic photographs ★

Dowling's Journey in a Coconut Shell

Today, Manila is the modern cultural and economic center of a fast growing metropolitan area with 10-million people and the highest population density of any major city in the world. It is the cosmopolitan capital and chief seaport of the Philippine Islands. Its parks and bay front are lined by new high-rise office and apartment buildings. It boasts of world-class shopping malls, theaters, entertainment and nightlife. Its radial roads and expressways are thronged with traffic and its crowded Ninoy Aquino International Airport is a crossroad of the Pacific, served by 38 airlines with flights worldwide. Signs everywhere display the brand names of familiar global companies. The main languages are Filipino (Tagalog) and American English, which is taught in all schools as a requirement for graduation. Because of its well-educated, skilled and English-speaking workforce, Manila is now a top outsourcing and call center location for companies engaged in e-commerce and business support.

But, it wasn't always so. In the year 1900, Manila was a dilapidated old Spanish city, occupied by the U.S. Army and still recovering from war. A city of magnificent churches surrounded by extreme poverty and factories employing child labor. It was a place where rebel prisoners had been thrown into a terrible "Black Hole" dungeon, tortured and executed while the wealthy lived behind high, gated walls, and promenaded the Luneta in ornate, horse-drawn carriages. The former colonial city had a population of perhaps 200,000 souls, but its streets were badly paved and badly lit. Sanitation was atrocious and diseases epidemic, including bubonic plague. What popular amusements there were centered around religious festivals, the lottery, pony races and cock fights. Spanish was the common language. Native huts were built on bamboo stilts over cesspools of filth and most buildings were not over 2-stories high.

America had "liberated" the islands from Spain, but inherited an ongoing native insurgency which nobody had expected and which seemed to have no ending. To make matters worse, 1900 was a presidential election year with the American public deeply divided on issues of imperialism, the policy of expansionism or independence for the islands. Many opposed the globalist policies of President William McKinley, charging that he was fighting the wrong war, in the wrong place and that it could never be won.

Then, in the midst of all the heated political controversy and rhetoric, Michael J. ("Jack") Dowling of Renville, Minnesota was asked by the McKinley Administration to go to the Philippines as an advance man ahead of the arrival of the Judge Taft Commission. Dowling's official instructions were to visit schools established by the U.S. Army and recommend a new system based on the American model of free education for every child. Unofficially, he was briefed by Secretary of War Elihu Root, and asked to gather any information or "stuff" he could learn about what the Filipinos were thinking, the intentions of the Sultan of Sulu or any signs that violence might spread.

Jack Dowling had been born with a radiant, optimistic personality. When he put on his wooden legs each morning, he also put on his smile. He had started teaching in a one room schoolhouse when he was not yet 21. "And, what a teacher he was!" Prudence Tasker Olson, a former student of Dowling's recalled that she learned world geography by hearing him tell "a wondrous tale in which John and his father were supposed to be traversing that strange country alone and on foot. This gave them time to examine the animals, the products, occupations, people, towns- it became more real to us than the room in which we sat." Dowling's letters from the Philippines tell similar tales of traveling through strange and far distant islands during a time of war and nation-building.

He was given a confidential briefing at the War Department and then traveled from Washington, D.C. to California, alone by rail, stopping in Los Angeles to visit a few exclusive men's clubs and take a carriage ride through Griffith Park with Colonel Griffith J. Griffith. At 12:05 P.M. on February 17, 1900 he climbed aboard ship in San Francisco. It was his birthday. He was 34-years old and the last passenger to go aboard. In a letter written at sea to "My dear Ones At Home" he cautioned his beautiful wife Jennie to keep SECRET the fact that he was traveling on the USAT Sherman, an Army troopship.

He had been assigned stateroom 3C on the promenade deck, starboard side, forward above the dining room, where he occupied the head of Table 4 during meals. Others around the table included Mr. Comfort who was to be in charge of the quarantine station at Manila; Mr. Nieson who was to run a commissary on Luzon; Major Lucey who was a paymaster clerk in the Army and four others, all postal clerks, going out to establish mail routes and a system of railway mail.

The voyage to the Philippines was "nasty, cold, stormy and rough." The Sherman was out of sight of land and did not see a sail or island for almost four weeks. She had no way to keep in touch with land or get news at sea. "You can't imagine how anxious we all are to find out what has been going on in the world...We discuss the Indian question, the Philippines, a standing army, the Boar-British war, the bubonic plague and nearly everything you can think of, but we know nothing at all," Dowling wrote.

Much of the time it was dangerous to walk about the deck. "The ship was pitching fearfully, and the waves were from 20-to 30-feet high. The screws were thrown out of the water every few minutes." He was aft on the quarter deck when a huge wave struck the ship, knocking people down. Jack had to brace his wooden legs and wrap an arm around a railing as he hung on for dear life. "The sailor lookout on Forecastle Bridge was swept off and for a few minutes it was thought he went overboard, but he was found hanging on a rope and rescued, though with two broken ribs and a bruised hand. I sought my stateroom for safety and stayed there where it was hard to sleep because I seemed to be standing first on my head and then on my stumps in the bunk." A few days later another storm did considerable damage to ventilators, canvas and iron railings about the decks. At times, Dowling found it was all he could do to get to the dining room and once he had to have a cabin boy come and give him an arm before he could make it down the steps.

Three hundred soldiers were berthed below decks in tiers of 3-high canvas racks with only a single blanket per man. All but 4 of the soldiers were seasick. In addition, the Sherman carried an assortment of passengers, most of whom were military or government employees or contractors headed for jobs in the Philippines. They included bookkeepers, managers, an interpreter, nurses, doctors and there was even an undertaker on board, plus a troupe of Filipino circus performers returning home from an appearance in the United States. When a black-haired baby girl was born to one of the women acrobats, the Captain declared the baby a U.S. citizen born on Washington's Birthday under the flag of the U.S. on a government ship on the high seas. And the proud parents named her Martha Washington Tabonis. A few days later, a stowaway was discovered, a 9-year old boy who told Dowling he was going to sell papers until he was old enough to join the Navy. "That's the love of the sea for you!" Dowling declared.

Weather permitting, Jack took Spanish lessons for 2- hours a day and spent the rest of the time climbing around, exploring every part of the ship, making friends with passengers and crew, playing pinochle and hearts, watching the flying fish and "gooney" birds, reading books and writing long letters home which, of course, could not be mailed until the ship reached port. He never missed a meal and was never seasick.

The Sherman arrived in Manila on March 14, and Dowling promptly reported to the Army commander General Elwell S. Otis, the very next day. The two men talked in SECRET behind closed doors, so we will never know for certain what was discussed. Dowling told Jennie that he was received "right regally" and that Otis gave him lots of good information. Both agreed that education would be the ultimate solution of the Philippine problem. Spreading American ideals through the schools would, in time, make good citizens of the Filipinos.

Otis described Manila as the "storm center" of the situation, but said the war was practically ended [*wrong*] and that no more troops were needed. Most of the islands were peaceful and quiet. On Luzon, however, bands of Christian Tagalo insurgents roamed the countryside, burning, looting and killing foreign traders and farmers. In mid-February, three Massachusetts soldiers had been captured, cruelly tortured and executed in the public plaza in Balinag. Tribes in the interior were pagan savages, some of whom had never seen a white man. Any travel beyond the army outposts around the capital could be dangerous. To date, the insurgency had cost America some 1,525 soldiers killed, or about 74 deaths per month.

General Otis was a veteran Indian fighter and bore a scar from the Civil War. Some in the newspapers had denounced the general for his strategy of clearing and burning Filipino villages and charged he was obsessed with minor detail, out-of-touch and incompetent. Whether Dowling's mission was part of a political attempt to hasten a "change of generals" and head off political debate is merely speculation. Coincidentally, a few days after their second, SECRET closed door meeting, it was announced April 9 in Washington that the 62 -year old Otis would be brought home "at his own request," promoted to Major General and reassigned to an Army regional headquarters.

Meanwhile, Dowling had found a large, airy room at the Oriente

Hotel. There were no screens on the windows, but the huge 4-poster bed was hung with mosquito netting. Many contractors, journalists and other Americans were staying there also, including Miss Beebe Beam, a female correspondent for the SAN FRANCISCO EXAMINER, who had the room next door, had cut her hair, dressed like a man and carried a pistol! Dowling represented himself as simply a newspaper correspondent from Minnesota and refused to discuss his true mission with anyone, including the general's subordinates, whom he told Jennie were "upstarts." His articles for the MINNEAPOLIS JOURNAL and other newspapers provided an ideal smokescreen for what he was actually doing.

His work may have been undercover, but he was certainly noticeable! One of his first moves, after arriving in Manila, was to find a tailor shop and order a trio of tropical suits to be custom made for him. Two khaki and one white. He also purchased an English-style pith helmet. "I look like pictures you have seen of Stanley exploring Africa," he wrote to Jennie. "All of the kids in town know me and call me 'Le Grande Americano.'"

It was his first trip to the tropics. In fact his first trip outside the United States, and he found Manila intensely hot, humid, dirty, crowded and confusing, with a "babel of tongues." In spite of the fact that April was one of the hottest months, he was out and about from 7 o'clock in the morning until 6 or 7 at night, seeking information and visiting schools. His visits were mostly unannounced. Sometimes, he tramped along on his wooden legs and other times he rode in one of the carriages that were pulled by "very strong swift little ponies a trifle larger than Shetlands. The fare was 20 to 25-cents an hour. All business houses, including the post office, and excepting the saloons," he wrote, "close at 12:30 p.m. and would open again at 2 p.m. The natives and old residents take their siestas at this time. The small shops, the laborers, the Chinese coolies, the cab drivers and the Americans keep on hustling." Only once did he complain about the heat and the weight of his heavy artificial arm and harness.

Dowling heard from Catholic sources that there had been 2,167 elementary schools in the Philippines before the war. But he was unable to learn from any source how many had been re-opened by the Army. So, he focused his study on those in Manila, where he was kept busy for three weeks. On March 29, he wrote a 3-page personal letter to "My dear Jennie" warning her against taking Turkish baths in the winter time and telling about his SECRET background interview with Archbishop Chapelle. "You remember of course that he is the Pope's special representative out here and therefore has exceptional opportunities to learn about the situation from the Catholic Philipinos. I got some things... that I can report to the Secretary of War that the shrewd old fellow told me under pledge that I would not print it. This is just the stuff that the Sec'y. of War wants, so I'm getting together the threads..." (And Dowling underlined 'just the stuff'.) For some unknown reason, this interview was never mentioned in Dowling's letters to the MINNEAPOLIS JOURNAL, nor was it covered in his written report to the Secretary of War. It was almost as if it never happened.

In the history of the Philippines, there had been numerous uprisings against Spanish oppression, the brutality of Catholic priests and excessive rents and taxes assessed by the Church. The most recent struggle had come to an end when Emilio Aguinaldo, the Christian leader of the Tagalo insurgents was bribed to accept an $800,000 cash payment to leave the island and go into exile. But when Admiral Dewey landed troops in Manila, Aguinaldo returned from exile, declared himself "dictator" of the islands and demanded complete and immediate independence. When that was refused, he tried to burn Manila and incited his Tagalo followers to kill Americans.

Dowling believed that U.S. military rule should give way to civil administration of Manila as quickly as possible, and that negotiations with Filipino leaders would soon bring peace. But, a major stumbling block was the insurgents' impossible demand for complete expulsion of all Spanish Catholic friars from the island. Under Spanish rule, the church had been granted vast holdings of land and governed many aspects of life. Most schools had been taught by priests who also acted as government agents with power to register all births, deaths and marriages. The dilemma Dowling faced was how to remove Catholic symbols and teaching from public schools while at the same time winning support from priests to help stop the insurgency and not losing support of Catholic voters at home. Control of the schools was a central issue for most Catholics.

And so, Dowling strode about Manila on his wooden legs, tramping through narrow alleyways and dark passages, trudging past horse stables and open sewers, dodging hogs and chickens, children and dogs and climbing stairs to second-story classrooms as he visited every one of the 41 public elementary schools in Manila. A 45-star American flag was flying over every building.

Always optimistic and looking ahead, Dowling envisioned a large-scale American aid program to replace all of the existing buildings and create a model system of schools serving every district of Manila. The cost would be considerable, he knew, but annual appropriations for operating could be levied as a local tax. An "educational force" of American teachers could be brought in to help staff the classrooms and the grounds of each new building planned to be over two acres in size and by law at least 300-feet from any saloon or "licensed" house of prostitution. There needed to be room for children to play in safety.

A big, school construction project would be a grand gesture of progress towards peace and would result in bright new classrooms furnished with good desks and provided with modern wall maps, textbooks in English and pictures of the type found in schools in the United States. Dowling reasoned that new schools, with "Americanized" classrooms, would be a complete change and thus be more respectful of the parents, priests and native teachers than a heavy handed removal of religious symbols from the old buildings.

Jack Dowling was a devoted husband and father, loved children and doted on his own baby daughter, Dorothy. Thus, he was both amused and appalled by what he saw in the Manila schools. "It was all I could do to keep my face straight," he wrote to Jennie, "while one girls' school sang for me 'My Country tis ob dee etc.' They have not got good voices, though they could play all manner of instruments and some schools have pianos." He found the toilet arrangements at most schools "something awful. The boys and girls just step outside the door... to attend to nature."

With his work in Manila finished, Dowling thought about visiting China and calling upon his friend and fellow Minnesotan, John Goodnow, who was the U.S. Consul in Shanghai and had a key role in the China situation. But, the voyage promised to be rough and conditions in China dangerous, so Dowling worked a last minute change of plans and embarked, April 4, on the USAT Pennsylvania which was headed down to the islands of Panay and Cebu and beyond. This new itinerary must have been personally arranged by General Otis and was probably intended to let Dowling see not only the Army's attention to civic projects, public works, local government and schools, but also the remote jungle islands where America was attempting to assimilate on Islamic society.

The Pennsylvania was a small vessel, but the largest supply ship operated among the islands by the Army Quartermaster Corps. The duration of the planned voyage was unknown. Dowling expected it might be anywhere from two to six weeks, but a fine opportunity to gather "stuff" for the Secretary of War, see more of the islands and, most importantly, try to interview the powerful Sultan of Sulu. If he succeeded, it would be the first important interview by any American journalist with that mysterious Muslim leader.

The island of Panay was the first stop. It was 332 miles from Manila and best known for growing and processing sugar cane. The port city of Iloilo was low, muddy and hot. The city had been cleared of insurgents, but left in ruins when fighting ended. Many buildings were blackened and gutted by fire, including the only school. The Pennsylvania unloaded a cargo of lumber for re-construction. And, Dowling wrote a very nice travel article for the MINNEAPOLIS JOURNAL about native fishing ponds, the Army canteen, the magnificent Catholic Church at Molo and the fine needlework of the sisters at their convent.

But, his letter home to "My dear Jennie" dated 13 April 1900 divulged some very different details. "The burial corps is loading on the last of 93 bodies that they have dug up for shipment to the states. We have had a tedious time," he wrote.

On Good Friday, he noticed that all American flags were flying at half mast. "I think it [*lowering flags for a religious holiday*] is a mistake that our government is making," he wrote.

One morning, there were loud gunshots aboard ship. "An insane soldier started in to kill all of us," Dowling told Jennie. "He had a 38-calibre revolver and a pocket full of cartridges with which to do it. He fired five shots before he was caught by a sergeant. I tell you there was some tall scrambling among us as he was in among our staterooms." The man demolished things, put on an officer's uniform, tossed things about, shaved his head, smashed a mirror, rifled through drawers and then commenced shooting. At one point, the man sat down between Dowling and a woman passenger on the saloon deck and said that he had "been having lots of fun."

Just before leaving Iloilo, a very sick soldier, "dying of dysentery" was put aboard for evacuation to Manila. Dowling hoped "the trip and happiness of coming will do him some good."

Feeling the anchor coming up and hearing three blasts of the ship's whistle, Dowling put aside his letter to Jennie, to be finished later, and went on deck with his fine pearl opera glasses to view the scenery as the ship steamed away and left Iloilo astern. He felt as though he had witnessed enough of the frightful cost of war in lives, bodies and minds.

Next morning, the ship dropped anchor at Cebu, where the welcome was in bright contrast to the dark days spent at Iloilo. Here, the Pennsylvania was immediately surrounded by about a dozen canoes filled with naked boys and girls who smiled, waved, called, sang songs and dove for coins tossed into the water by soldiers and passengers. "I like this place better than any I have seen so far," Dowling decided.

The commanding officer, Colonel E.J. McClernand soon "came on board and took dinner or 'tiffen' with us" wrote Dowling. The Colonel was a West Point graduate who had fought in the Indian Wars and been awarded the Congressional Medal of Honor. He had successfully defeated Arcadio Maxilom, taken Cebu's ports and cities for the United States and driven the remnants of the local insurgency into the mountains.

However, he warned that Cebu was still a dangerous place and that soldiers were sometimes fired upon, even within the city. Nobody would be allowed beyond the outskirts without a military escort of at least eight armed soldiers. The Visayan "insurrectos" had fortified themselves a few miles away and were armed with rifles and bolos. A few days ago, two soldiers who strayed beyond the lines had been killed and literally cut to pieces. Dowling was a little miffed when the Colonel refused him permission to visit or sail around the coral island of Mactan, where the explorer Magellan had been killed in 1521.

Instead, the Colonel invited Dowling to attend what would be McClernand's first meeting with the native municipal government. He felt that Dowling should see how the Army was restoring the island to normal and helping peaceful natives to run their own affairs. Dowling noted that the city officials were "exceedingly anxious to have more school houses, equipped with American teachers and furniture, for which they expressed a willingness to tax themselves."

McClernand had written a piece for the NEW YORK TIMES and believed "the thorough defeat of the insurgents will not be the entire solution of the problem. And so, we are pursuing a strategy to win the peace by re-opening the ports, re-opening the schools and hastening the revival of industry and commerce. The inhabitants need to know that our flag is here to stay and that it is now their flag as well as ours."

Following the meeting with city officials, Dowling was taken on a tour of native housing areas where he saw poverty and filth, the like of which he had never experienced before. Under each nipa hut was a cesspool of filth surrounded by "chickens and dogs, children and hogs." All of which seemed in stark contrast to the Bishop's fine palace nearby, and the extravagant cathedrals and churches erected by generations of Spanish priests.

McClernand acknowledged that "The priests exercise great power and upon our arrival seemed disposed to stand aloof. *[Rumor had it that some were helping insurgents.]* But, now they are showing more willingness to unite their effort with ours to advance the good of the people. And, most of the people of Cebu are devout Catholics."

One day, while Dowling was in Cebu, the Commanding Officer personally visited all five of the city's public schools. Dowling may have ridden along for part of the tour. His official report to the Secretary of War dedicated a full page to the schools of Cebu.

"It is no easy matter," McClernand said, "to take up the government of people with a different civilization from ours, perhaps with only a semi-civilization and incorporate them. Americans will need immense patience, but the effort will be mutually beneficial in the end."

Most of the people on Cebu were Visayans as opposed to the Tagalos on Luzon and around Manila. The culture of the islands was deeply divided by ethnic, religious and tribal differences. At the time, there were about 80 different tribal groups, speaking some 60 different languages. Many of the tribes disliked the Tagalo and feared their rule if the insurgents were to win.

Cebu was a city of about 15,000 population, with three daily newspapers. Dowling managed to visit all of them, including one that was an anti-imperialist, anti-American start-up which had just published its first edition. Dowling found the editor and engaged him in a very frank and heated debate. The editor claimed that his paper had no link to the insurgents, but accused the Americans of bad faith and charged that the McKinley administration had always intended to take possession of the Philippines. He predicted that America would never be able to control the islands as long as a native lived who could get his hand on a bolo knife!

When asked about the new Taft Commission that would soon be governing the islands, Dowling said it would probably report conditions as they existed and recommend hanging of all natives who persisted in killing and robbing outposts. In other words, "it would call such men robbers and murderers and treat them as such." The angry editor insisted that "Freedom is what we want and our people will fight thirty years if necessary to secure it. When Byran is elected, he will give us our independence," he declared. Dowling thought this unlikely and found the man's view of U.S. politics amusing. Was this more "stuff" for the Secretary of War?

The town of Cebu was "well built and picturesque," but too hot for much tramping about and the streets were three or four inches deep in dust. Wading through it was "not a picnic." Dowling saw quite a bit of new construction going up. A contractor's representative for Vulcan Iron Works had come there on the Pennsylvania to build two ice plants in the city. One private, and one for the government.

On Easter Sunday, Dowling watched the Catholic Bishop go down the street as hundreds of natives crowded around to kiss his outstretched right hand. He wrote Jennie that the man was hugely overweight and wrinkled with fat. Dowling was also critical of the lavish amounts of money that had been spent building churches. The most famous was the Church of the Santo Nino, "the Holy Child of Cebu," which contained a sacred wooden relic. Natives came from all parts of the island to kneel before it. The processions in celebration of Easter were long and colorful and included native bands and music.

One day, Dowling missed the launch back to the ship and had to hire a small canoe with bamboo outriggers to bring him out. "It was a tippy little affair," he wrote Jennie, "and all the passengers and officers yelled with laughter when they saw me coming, bobbing up and down on the waves and swinging from one side to the other in imminent danger of going over."

A party of four in another canoe did tip over and the ship's boat had to be lowered to pick them up.

Zamboanga, on the island of Mindanao, was the next port of call. The ship arrived there April 21st, amidst the beauty of a tropical sunrise.

Here, in the southern Philippines, Dowling experienced his first contact with the Moro followers of Islam. He decided they looked "piratical" and had many strange customs. He was never entirely comfortable in their presence.

Their local leader, Dato Mandi, was a friend of Americans and had helped drive Vincente Alvarez and a force of Christian insurgents out of Zamboanga. This had enabled U.S. soldiers to occupy the capital city of the island without having to fire a shot.

The Dato or prince was 37-years old and had fathered 14 children with his three wives and an unknown number of concubines. Dowling visited him at his house, which was a fine building made of beautiful hardwood. He found the Dato to be intelligent and friendly and wrote that he was second only to the Sultan of Sulu in his power over the Moros.

War had not touched this part of the Philippines and relations with the population were "quiet and satisfactory" except for a few minor incidents among the Christian settlements in the most northern parts of the island. So it was quite safe for Dowling to climb on a saddle pony, and go riding out of the city for a day with Mr. Russell, the local superintendent of schools.

Dowling was an expert rider. He had been a kid cowboy at age 12, self-supporting and responsible for a herd of 500 cattle out on the open prairie. He had been around horses most of his life and could ride "almost anything on four legs." He owned a fine Kentucky thoroughbred riding horse "Prince" and a half broken team of "Billy" and "Kid," all safe in the pasture back home. But, it was still winter in Minnesota. He asked Jennie to "give the horses a hot bran mash and tell them it is from me." (It would be another three years before Dowling bought the first horseless carriage sold in Renville County and started calling himself "the mechanized man.")

He visited two schools on Mindanao and said the one at Tetuan, which had been built by the Army with native assistance, was the best schoolhouse in the Philippines. "Sanitary arrangements are excellent," he wrote," the grounds have been cleared of brush and trees; plants have been set out and climbing vines trained over the building. Altogether a homelike and attractive appearance." The children were Moros and Visayans. Although there were no school-books in English, Dowling commended the good work being done by the officer-in-charge, who told him every town in the province had two schools- one for boys and one for girls.

The 92 miles from Zamboanga to Jolo seemed very short. Dowling spent the morning watching fish, dolphins and the spouting of whales as the Pennsylvania cut through the mirror-like surface of the sea and cruised among the many, beautiful islands of the Sulu archipelago. At 2 p.m. on April 22, she anchored in the harbor at Jolo and he went ashore to sightsee and visit the schools.

He soon learned that a new, 2-story frame school building was being constructed there by soldiers commanded by a Major Owen Sweet. Location of the new building was outside the walled city and near the Moro village of Tulai. The wooden frame was up and completion of the building expected in another six weeks. When finished, the new school would be the Moro school for boys.

Inside the walled city of Jolo, classes were being taught in a basement room for a number of boys and girls, Filipinos, Moros, Mestizos, Chinese and Spanish. A man from Borneo was the teacher. He spoke English, Arabic, Maylay and Spanish. Dowling found the basement room to be damp and unhealthy, but he praised the teacher and his students, whom Dowling said, "read and write excellent English and recite intelligently in geography and mathematics."

The island of Jolo was controlled by a Muslim Sultan and perceived as one of the Philippines' most remote and dangerous places. Sultan Jamul-ul-Kiram II ruled there and also claimed territory in North Borneo. He traced his ancestry back to the prophet Mohammed, with blood ties stretching all the way to Mecca and also to the very influential Sultan of Turkey. All papers of state were written in Arabic. Coincidentally, or not, Dowling had arrived at a very critical time. Diplomatic relations with the Sultan of Turkey appeared to be breaking down. In a front page news story datelined New York, April 20, the MINNEAPOLIS JOURNAL reported:

> *"There are in the Philippines more than 3,500,000 Moslems, in the Sulu islands whose dedication to their caliph is fanatical. The sultan would have but to lift his finger and these Maylays and Moros would join forces with Tagalos. The war in Luzon would be extended in every direction and the American forces would necessarily have to be greatly increased."*

The importance of having the Sultan of Sulu as a friend and partner was one of the many things covered at Dowling's War Department briefing before his trip. The Sultan had signed the so-called "Bates Agreement" and supposedly acknowledged U.S. sovereignty in return for an annual stipend of $3,000 from Uncle Sam. But, the Sultan was still collecting his own taxes, enforcing Islamic laws and practicing polygamy and slavery as usual.

The intent of the Agreement was to gain control of Sulu ports, put a stop to piracy and prevent German and/or Japanese gun-runners from smuggling arms to insurgents by way of the "back door" to the Phlippines. Under its terms, America had to promise to respect the Islamic religion and the customs of the Moro population. But, the Agreement was NOT a formal treaty and could be broken whenever it became no longer convenient or politically acceptable. President McKinley had given it his limited approval, but reserved the issue of slavery for "future conference, determination and agreement." Notice of McKinley's approval was delivered to the Sultan just two weeks before Dowling reached Jolo.

Relations with the Sultan had been going nowhere since January, when ten Moros had been killed by the U.S. Army in the so-called Tragedy of Tawi-Tawi. The Sultan had wanted payment of $1,000 in gold for each of the victims. (As much as $1-million in today's money.) But, he had withdrawn his wildly inflated demand when threatened with a possible counter-claim for American lives lost.

When Dowling learned that Sultan Kiram II had come over to the Moro village and was collecting taxes there, he knew he had to get an interview. But, the Pennsylvania was in port just overnight and scheduled to put to sea again the very next evening. He would have only one chance to see the feared Muslim ruler.

Dowling was told it could be taking his life in his hands (if he had his hands) to approach the Sultan by surprise or without a proper appointment. But, Jack was desperate to get an interview, whatever the risk might be.

"Don't worry about me," he joked, "I used to live in Chicago!"

Hadn't his father taught him to be a bare knuckle fighter? And, hadn't he once captured an armed, street bandit in Colorado by clubbing the would-be thief with his wooden arm? So, with two soldiers for escorts, Dowling ventured beyond the safety of the walled city to find the house where the Sultan was receiving his gold.

Dowling's eighth letter to the MINNEAPOLIS JOURNAL tells of being surrounded by about 30 of the Sultan's armed bodyguards; seating himself and watching the outlandish proceedings for an hour and a half; at last pushing his chair into the room where his highness was busy chewing betel nut and accepting payment and finally disrupting the Sultan's dealings by displaying his wooden limbs and raising his arms as if to unscrew his head! Behavior which certainly caught the Sultan's attention and brought the bodyguards rushing in. Luckily for Dowling, the Moro ruler began to laugh heartily, quit seeing taxpayers, summoned an interpreter and said, "Keep your head on! I want to talk with you. I want to talk with the wooden man."

Nobody will ever know what actually passed between Dowling and the Sultan during that incredible interview. But, living on a warm, tropical island, the Sultan must have listened in wonder and disbelief as the man from Minnesota told of the freezing blizzard which had cost him his legs and hands. Questions of money, schools and the American occupation would also have been discussed. But, why did Dowling pull his leg and make such a phenomenal attempt to get that interview?" Was it about "stuff" for the Secretary of War?

When the Sultan declared that Uncle Sam was not paying him enough for the American occupation of Sulu, nor for his continued friendship and goodwill, Dowling brushed it aside, telling the Sultan that $250 a month was considered a good thing and $50 more than Spain had paid. At heart, Dowling believed the Sultan was "lazy, vindictive and selfishly greedy...a most unworthy king."

Dowling chose instead to focus on the benefits of modern education and the building of new schools, like the one under construction by Major Sweet. "Papa Sweet is a good man," the Sultan agreed, "and he is winning the hearts of my people." Dowling kept silent, but knew what Sweet really wanted was to abolish the Muslim sultanate and do away with slavery and polygamy. Nor did Dowling want to explain that religious instruction would be kept out of public schools.

Jack Dowling was a winning salesman who knew the best way to sell a grand idea or vision! He would say with enthusiasm that modern education wasn't just about new buildings or English textbooks. A good American education was the open doorway to a golden future of wonderful opportunities! "Ten years of American schooling will work wonders," Dowling exclaimed as he described a new educational system for the islands that would drive out the old Spanish method of memorization and teach children to think, concentrate and learn. He recalled that it was first and foremost the chance for a good education which had given his own life such a renewed sense of hope and optimism. "Philippine students are bright and will surprise the world with their progress and skills. All they need to open the door to opportunity are new buildings, new schoolbooks and a force of the best qualified American and native teachers that can be found."

The Sultan replied that he wanted whatever was good for his people and that he would send his sons to school to become wise leaders. He promised to assist with building new schools, but only for his Moro and Maylay followers. If it became known that he cooperated too closely with the Americans, it might risk assassination.

Before Dowling left, he was shown the harem and offered his choice of the women, which he politely refused. Among the souvenirs which he did bring home was a gruesome "beheading sword" (or "kris") which was kept for many years on a high shelf in the dining room of the Dowling home, safely out of reach of children playing "pirates."

The "Pennsy" left Jolo late in the evening and dropped anchor off the island of Bangao in the Tawi-Tawi group at 12 Noon, April 25. A wildly enthusiastic welcome greeted her arrival. A small boatload of soldiers came out to meet the ship's launch. All of the men were cheering and calling and waving their hats. The little Army garrison on that far distant island had been without visitors and cut off from any news of the outside world for 6-weeks. At last, the Pennsylvania had come, bringing not only mail from home, but also a shipment of beer!

The small Army outpost was closer to Borneo than to Manila and manned by a single company of American 23rd Infantry soldiers. The troops had built their own quarters and were encamped in Nipa huts erected on numbered lots along both sides of the company street. The troops had also built a library and hospital, but no schoolhouse. Dowling felt it would be easy to establish a school and that the Army doctor might be a good teacher.

For the first time in his travels, Dowling wrote about the lives of enlisted soldiers. The loneliness and boredom faced by sergeants and privates while awaiting the unknown terrors of war. Their excitement upon receiving mail. Dowling's previous articles were more about opportunities for business and trade and read more like travelogs than like dispatches from a war zone. He had little use for upstarts at Army headquarters or for rear echelon, garrison soldiers who never found the time to learn about Manila or its people. He called them "would-be heros looking for sympathy" when they complained of hardships and dangers. He chafed at Army restrictions and disliked officers with "more shoulder straps and less brains."

But, his letter from Bangao to the MINNEAPOLIS JOURNAL includes some horrific details about the so called "tragedy of Tawi-Tawi" as heard directly from the men involved. In January 1900, Sergeant DeWolfe, Corporal Mygatt and Privates Gibbons, Carter and Gatehouse of Company H, 23rd Infantry had been taken by surprise while on a 7-day outing at a lake on Tawi-Tawi. DeWolfe and Gibbons were hacked to death by Moros, but the others escaped. Captain Sydney Cloman had demanded the nearby village surrender the murderers, who apparently killed for no other reason than to steal the soldiers' rifles. Ten suspects were delivered into Army custody and later shot dead while allegedly trying to escape. Dowling felt the outcome created respect for American soldiers and was one of the best things that could have happened. He found that Captain Cloman had done nothing wrong. Dowling said that Cloman was worshipped by his men and he personally liked him best of any officer he had met so far! Dowling's opinions would be seen as very controversial, if not racist by today's standards.

The Moros of Bongao, Tawi-Tawi and several smaller islands in the vicinity were governed by two Datos who ruled under the Sultan and paid him tribute. News of the "wooden man" had spread by jungle telegraph among the islands, so Dowling was not surprised when Dato Tanton showed up on

Bangao to see his artificial limbs and asked, "If all of the Americans in the district in which I lived were built like me?"

Dowling was also fascinated by stories of the fabulous "Black Pearl of Bangao," which was said to be as large as a chicken's egg, a perfect sphere with fine luster, and owned by the Sultan of Sulu. He believed that fortunes were being made in the pearl fisheries of Bangao, even though all pearls above a certain size had to be paid to the Sultan.

After completing its 1,759-mile voyage among the islands, the Pennsylvania arrived back at Manila the evening of April 30, only to learn that fighting around the city the previous week had been the bloodiest of the war. In that week alone, 378 Filipinos had been killed along with 9 American soldiers dead and 16 others wounded. With disease also rampant in the city and his mission successfully finished, Dowling had seen the Philippines from "top to bottom" and was ready to go home.

Before leaving, Dowling paid his respects to the 73-year old mother of the martyred Filipino patriot, Dr. Jose Rizal. His final letter to the MINNEAPOLIS JOURNAL dated Manila P.I. May 1, 1900 was all about the life of Dr. Rizal, and his execution by the Spaniards and was a wonderfully warm and well written tribute to his memory. It was also the only one of Dowling's articles that was illustrated.

Dr. Jose Rizal was a doctor of medicine and philosophy, a literary genius, a poet, a published author, an artist, a sculptor and fluent in eleven languages as well as thirteen different Filipino dialects. The blind, the deaf, the dumb and the lame were brought to him in huge numbers for treatment.

Dowling called Rizal "the brightest intellectual light that has shown from the dense darkness of Filipino ignorance." and, Rizal's mother said, "If my son had lived there never would have been an insurrection against the authority of the United States. He believed the American people to be the best governed and most just nation among all the governments of the world."

Dowling drew a sharp distinction between patriots like Dr. Rizal and those Filipino brigands and bandits who lived by plunder. He was also harshly critical of the Sultan of Sulu and his life-style. But such was the American dilemma. How to bring modern civilization to the Philippines without resorting to unthinkable violence or unending war? Dowling's plan was to transform the schools. He believed that American-style education, combined with very great patience, would open the way to a bright future.

On May 5, Dowling packed his trunks and then sat and watched while troops marched into formation, a military band played and a ceremony was held as General Otis read his orders, transferred command of troops in the Philippines to General Arthur McArthur and left his post. Then the band played "Auld Lang Syne" as soldiers of the 20th and 14th infantry came to attention to "present arms" and the shore battery of cannon fired a salute to the departing general.

As one of his last official acts, General Otis had appointed Captain Todd as Superintendent of schools for the Philippine archipelago. But the appointment was largely symbolic window dressing, since most of the public schools would soon come under civil control and there would be no more soldier school teachers.

Some newspapers questioned the timing of the general's departure and asked why Otis didn't wait for the expected June 3 arrival of the Taft Commission which was on its way to begin the establishment of a civilian government. Other papers, such as the MANILA AMERICAN, criticized that Otis left a lot unfinished, "but he left the islands, and that is the main thing."

After the ceremony, both Dowling and Otis boarded the USAT Meade and steamed for home, Otis was quartered in a special, high-ranking suite (flag cabin) while Dowling was assigned a regular officer's stateroom. Reticent by nature, Otis probably didn't take his meals with the other passengers, but was served meals in his cabin, Dowling, on the other hand, would have visited with everybody, played cards and sang and been the jovial center of conversation.

The 25-day voyage home across the Pacific was apparently routine and uneventful until reaching San Francisco, on May 30, when the entire ship was ordered into quarantine and nobody allowed to land until June 4, one day after the Taft Commission reached Manila. Three cases of smallpox had been discovered among the troops below decks. Dowling had returned healthy, but 30-pounds lighter and was in no danger of contracting the disease as he had been vaccinated going over. Still, he was very frustrated by the delay and may have been quoting Otis when he telegrammed the MINNEAPOLIS JOURNAL "One Army officer of high rank, seeing the doctors mingling freely with the cabin passengers after examining patients said, 'the quarantine officers seem determined to infect us and keep us here to witness their success.'"

Upon release from quarantine, Dowling checked into the Palace Hotel in San Francisco where he stayed briefly, picked up his mail and happened to meet the playwright, George Ade and told him of his adventures in the Philippines. According to newspaper accounts, "Mr. Ade immediately took out one of his visiting cards and wrote on it:

> Admit the bearer, Michael J. Dowling, to the first performance of the Sultan of Sulu!
> And that is how the famous comic opera came to be written"

At this point, Dowling had been traveling for almost 5 months and longed to return to Jennie and his "own little home in Renville." But, first he needed to hurry on to Washington, D.C. ("which Renville people must know nothing about") then home. But, why such a rush to report in person to Secretary Elihu Root? And why in SECRET?

Dowling had gathered lots of "stuff" to tell Root and had a very clear plan in mind to transform the schools of Manila. But, his formal report entitled "Education in the Philippines" would not be ready for another six-weeks. His final 23-page report was completed July 13, 1900 and typewritten by Jennie's sister, Hattie Bordewich, on the same manual typewriter that Dowling had used when he edited a weekly newspaper, purchased the first typewriter ever seen in the village and taught himself to type "no handed."

The Dowling Report was a very detailed and objective evaluation of existing schools as to buildings, school furniture, teachers, pupils and parents. It was focused on Manila first and steps needed to create a model school system in that important city. But, he also detailed his findings on other islands. There was no mention of the Sultan of Sulu or any of the "stuff" that he learned for the Secretary of War. In conclusion, Dowling summarized his recommendations on education as follows:

> *"Emphasize the teaching of English, ignore religion, establish manual training schools and a temporary normal school (i.e., teachers' college), select a corps of first class American teachers, pay them well and build model schools in Manila thereby creating a standard for emulation."*

As important as the Dowling Report may have seemed at the time, it wasn't everything the Army wanted to hear. Dowling gave most of the schools in Manila low marks and graded all of the buildings "unsatisfactory." He found the superintendent, Rev. G.P. Anderson, had little or no experience and lacked the ability, diplomacy and judgment necessary in that position. He recommended that Anderson be replaced by someone from the U.S. with experience in management of a city school system.

With a presidential election fast approaching, the Dowling Report was never publicized or released to the press. But, it provided a clear blueprint which was quickly implemented by the Taft commission. While not all of his recommendations were adopted right away, within less than 60-days the Taft commission began to erect modern school buildings, sent for a force of American teachers and planned to start an exchange program to send Filipino teachers to visit schools in the United States and tour Washington, D.C.

The following year, in 1901, the Congress appropriated $40,000 for a normal and trade school in Manila and $15,000 for an agricultural station on the island of Negros. The cost of buildings was authorized at $400,000. The Act also defined school policy on religion as Dowling had recommended. Religious classes were allowed, but only three days a week and only after regular school hours. Dowling received a formal letter of appreciation and thanks from Secretary Root, dated July 24, 1900 and believed that all of his recommendations had been adopted.

However, Dowling realized that even with people eager to learn and a modern school system, starting in the lower grades, it would be a generation or longer before the islands could begin to see results in higher incomes or a rising standard of living. Eventually a new "Americanized" middle class of well-educated, skilled adults would create new jobs and change the very fabric of the islands' culture and society. Clearly, it was the beginning of a new era, but nobody could imagine the incredible changes the future would bring.

Education had been the centerpiece of President McKinley's policy of benevolent assimilation. Re-opening and building schools was an idea supported by everybody, both in the Army and the Administration. Dowling was an unsung hero whose vision and plan for a system of free public schools in the Philippines resulted in more goodwill and understanding than could have been accomplished by any other means. It demonstrated America's good intentions and helped defeat a violent insurgency which could have led to dictatorship or catastrophe. Dowling strongly believed that "There is no such thing as a cripple if the mind is right." By his own example, Michael J. Dowling showed how one person, even "leg-less and arm-less," could with courage and determination, make a difference, help others and shape the future. He may have been a "wooden man," but he certainly didn't have a wooden head.

He was not a cripple!

Editor's Note:

After Dowling returned from the Philippines he ran for the Minnesota state legislature and won election by a large margin. In January 1901 he was chosen speaker of the house.

THE DOWLING FAMILY 1899

Jack wrote long letters home to his dear wife, Jennie and baby daughter, Dorothy. Hattie Bordewich, Jennie's unmarried younger sister, also boarded with the family. She worked for Dowling as his personal secretary and close business and political associate.

He greatly missed his family and little home in Renville. In a letter dated Manila, March 26, 1900 he wrote, "How I would like to see that blessed little baby Dorothy! I long and long for her and when I say this I mean her mother as well. I feel that you are all well but this is a long ways from you in case you should need me..."

"Just think of 8000 miles and boats only once in two weeks and continuous going would require a month to get to you ... tell them all that I plan to be home for the 4th of July. With lots of love and hugs and kisses I am ever your loving Jack. Hello Dorothy! Can you hear papa call you?"

CAMPAIGNING FOR PRESIDENT WILLIAM MCKINLEY

Pictured is President William McKinley (left) with Michael J. Dowling (right) and John Goodnow (center). Both Dowling and Goodnow were from Minnesota and good friends. Goodnow was U.S. Consul General at Shanghai and a strong supporter of administration policy in the "Open Door" negotiations with China. It was believed at the time that the Philippine Islands were key to protection of American interests in the Orient. Therefore, Dowling's mission to the islands came at a very critical time because if Aguinaldo and the insurgents fought on, the islands could breakdown into chaos and mass killings of Christians and foreigners as was happening in China with the so-called "Boxer Rebellion."

A HEAVY ARM
AN UNCOMFORTABLE LEG

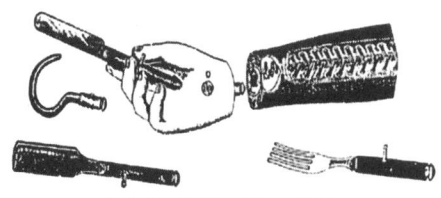

Showing tools used in Artificial Hand and Wrist

In Manila, during what was the hottest season of the year, Dowling had to get about with two artificial legs and an artificial arm. "The harness of which," he wrote, "is heavy and lacking in every essential tendency towards coolness of attire." Still he walked in the hot sun visiting all the city and talking with people from every trade or profession. He toured a piano factory, a prison, a cigar and cigarette factory, various newspapers, an insane asylum, churches, a new cold-storage building and every public school in the city. March 29 he wrote that he had "an uncomfortable leg" where he had rubbed the skin off. At right are drawings of his artificial limbs.

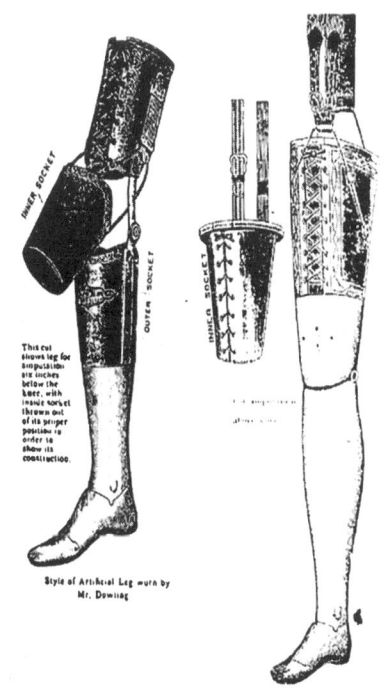

Style of Artificial Leg worn by Mr. Dowling

SUPPORTING THE TROOPS

Jack Dowling was an impassioned patriot and inspiring orator. In this photograph we see him "enthusing" a crowd in support of Army Volunteers departing for service in the Spanish-American War.

When hostilities began, in April 1898, Dowling wrote to President McKinley and volunteered to help the war effort in any way possible. But, his letter was referred to the Secretary of War and nothing came of it until almost two years later.

Then, suddenly, Dowling was asked by Secretary of War Elihu Root to go to the Philippines on a one-man government mission to study the school system and report his findings. Transportation and meals would be furnished, but he would have to pay for everything else. If he accepted, it meant he would have to travel into a dangerous war zone where American troops were still taking casualties and battling a brutal insurgency.

Dowling quickly agreed to take the appointment and went to Washington, D.C. for a Confidential briefing. Then he retired as President of the Renville Bank and made plans for the voyage.

LEGS OF BASSWOOD AND STEEL

This is photograph of M.J. Dowling with his trousers rolled up to show his artificial legs. The picture was taken in 1902 by the Winkley Artificial Limb Co. of Minneapolis.

Dowling rarely showed his legs, declaring, "If you have a handicap, try to act as if you hadn't. Try to forget it yourself. And, above all things, don't let other people keep it in their minds."

Here we see him with a cigar in his mouth, a full mustache and hardly a shadow of a beard. He was of medium height, trim in his 30's. Had reddish brown hair.

He traveled wherever he pleased without a companion. He never needed one to look after him. He refused to look back or pity himself. He was always optimistic and self reliant. When he put on his legs each morning, he also put on his smile!

THE TRAVELING MAN

Michael J. Dowling as he looked while criss-crossing the country as Secretary of the National Republican League. People he met did not see a man with a handicap. They saw a man who stood straight, looked them in the face with twinkling blue eyes and greeted them with a smile.

He often said that his handicap was God's greatest gift, because it forced him to think and work and win as he never had before. Dowling seldom talked about it and never used it to obtain special favors. He had a wife, family, friends, business and a dozen other interests. He was well and strong. And he never waited for luck to find him. He went out after it!

One summer, he traveled all through Minnesota, Iowa and Nebraska writing insurance. He was so persuasive that some believed he could "sell burned boards." In fact, as a child, he had actually sold burned boards as relics and souvenirs of the great Chicago fire.

U.S.A. Transport "Sherman."

ABOARD AN ARMY TRANSPORT

The USAT Sherman was one of five British ships purchased by the U.S. Army and converted into troopships during the Spanish-American War. She was built originally as a cattle boat and launched at Belfast, Ireland in 1893. There was no laundry on board. Length was 445-feet. Beam 50-feet. Tonnage 5,780. She had a single stack, four masts and a single screw. The Sherman had a speed of 12-knots and operated during 1900 on a regular monthly schedule between San Francisco and Manila. Her commander at the time was Captain C.H. Grant and most of the crew were Norwegian. The Sherman later participated in the Boxer Rebellion and World War I. The ship also took part in the first ship-to shore demonstration of working "wireless signals" in America.

ON A STREET IN MANILA

Michael Dowling went around Manila dressed in white and wearing an English-style helmet. Here we see him in front of a government building with the 45-star American flag flying overhead. "I look like picture you have seen of Stanley exploring Africa," he told Jennie. "All of the kids in town know me and call me 'Le Grande Americano.' I find that I know more about Manila as a whole than officers or privates who have been here a year or more," he criticized, "because I have been making it my business to see it." And, see most of it he did, as he managed to personally inspect all 41 of the city's elementary public schools.

ELECTRICITY COMES TO MANILA

In 1900, only a few parts of Manila were lighted by electricity. Many streets, especially in the old, walled town, were lighted by kerosene lamps or wicks suspended in dishes of coconut oil. Here, contractors are shown, working to erect power poles along the Pasig River to extend electricity to what Dowling said was "the first large cold-storage building which Uncle Sam has nearly finished for the purpose of furnishing fresh meats, eggs, milk and butter for the soldiers. It is one of the finest buildings in the city and will have a machine for the manufacture of ice and the freezing of food." Refrigerator ships from Australia regularly arrived in Manila to unload cargoes of meats.

Selling from a bull cart.

Street peddlers.

STREET SELLERS IN MANILA

Jack Dowling was born "poor, but Irish" and knew the life of a "street seller." He was with his parents in Chicago during the great fire that burned the city. Afterwards, his father found him digging in the ruins for blackened "relics" which he could sell to souvenir hunters. At age 10, he was on the streets of Chicago, peddling papers as a newsboy by day and selling flowers in front of theaters by night. But, the street sellers of Manila were unlike any he had seen before. Some balanced baskets of fruit on their heads, others sold their wares from "bull carts" or from hole-in-the-wall shop stalls. The oranges were fair, bananas small, but good, mangoes very nice, chicos sickish sweet, coconuts two-cents each and fine cigars ten-cents. Many natives seemed to be only half clothed. "They wash themselves a great deal," Dowling wrote, "but, it is to cool themselves, not to keep clean." He had been taught since childhood to always "keep his hands clean in every way."

COCK FIGHTING FOR SPORT

It seemed that every Filipino native owned a fighting cock. These large and raucous birds usually had the run of the family house and even roosted overhead among the rafters. People joked that in case of fire, men would save their battling birds before their own children. Here we see a photograph of natives with their fighting roosters. Large sums of money were waged on cock fights, but individual bets could not exceed $50. The sport was controlled and taxed by the government and allowed only on Sundays and certain special occasions.

A PHILIPPINE WATER BUFFALO

Before trucks or bulldozers, there were Philippine water buffalo. These great beasts of burden were used for every kind of work from logging to hauling carts with heavy loads of sugar cane. Buffalo were plodding and awkward animals, but long-lived, responsive and easily trained. However, they needed to be bathed at least once a day or after working a couple of hours in the heat of the day. Children could ride them bareback and control them with a string and piece of split rattan in the nostrils of the animal. Filipinos loved their buffalo like Americans loved their horses.

BOYS NEED MANUAL TRAINING

Dowling believed that a "manual training school is next in importance to a free public school." He especially recommended that a manual training school should be established in Manila, where boys could work with their hands, learn woodworking skills and practice the use of tools. Here we see a class of boys with their native teacher in the back row. The photograph was probably taken in Cebu. While most boys were well dressed, a few came to school wearing only a shirt or a kind of string around the waist. At one school, Dowling saw a boy smoking a cigarette in class. At another, the teacher was smoking. But, discipline of children in some cases was very severe. Dowling disapproved of that. Native teachers were paid $14 Mexican per month. Americans averaged $50 gold. April and May were normally vacation months due to the heat and seasonal diseases.

GIRLS LEARNED SEWING AND NEEDLEWORK

Girls and boys attended separate schools, but none had large, safe areas where children could play outside. Girls relaxed from studies by doing some "very good sewing" including plain and fancy needlework and embroidery. All of the girls were very young, but clean, neatly dressed and eager to learn. Dowling found one little girl, a 7-year-old prodigy, who could read English fluently, recite poems and write as well as an American child 10-years of age. However, only a small percentage of children (perhaps one fifth) attended school at all. Sickness was widespread and most dropped out by age 12. Classes were dismissed and everyone, teachers and pupils, took a "siesta" during the heat of the day.

AN ARMY WAGON ON CEBU

Provisions for American troops had to be hauled by horse and wagon to outpost camps. Commissary trains or convoys came under frequent attack. This photograph shows an Army wagon and its escort of soldiers. Man up on the wagon box with the driver (back row, left) may be Dowling. The officer next to him could be Colonel McClernand. The picture appears to have been taken in front of a school building as the two men visited schools and outposts around Cebu together. Dowling had learned to shoot and ride while working as a kid cowboy on a ranch in Wyoming and once was the only man in his hunting party to down a moose. In this picture, he is probably just holding a rifle for the man who snapped the photograph. Dowling had forgotten to bring his Kodak to the Philippines.

INSURGENTS ON THE MOUNTAINTOPS

American troops drove insurgents out of this mountaintop position on Cebu just a month before Dowling arrived. Native Filipinos were very dangerous with their bolos and spears and fighting was often hand-to-hand in close combat with bayonets and gun butts. Rain was frequent and temperature mostly in the nineties. There were no roads or bridges in the mountainous interior. Soldiers sometimes marched at night in knee deep mud or had to cross deep rivers on rope cables, only to find a village empty and the insurgents fled to hiding. Soldiers used the shacks to rest up in, and then burned them down and moved on. Later, bands of insurgents would return to fight from ambush, hiding along roadsides and killing travelers or other natives and farmers thought to be helping Americans. They also raided and burned plantations and harassed garrisons in coastal ports. U.S. strategy was to route the insurgents, capture their arms and ammunition and blockade the islands so they could not be re-supplied.

SULTAN JAMAL-UL-KARIM II

The Sultan of Sulu (front row center) and his close advisors posed for this rare photograph in 1899. The Sultan's bloodling traced back to the prophet Muhammad. He had two wives, thirteen concubines and also owned a number of slaves. He received tribute from various local Datos or princes and also profited from the islands' lucrative pearl fisheries. The Sultan wore no beard and followed a Maylay branch of Islam. The American officer was 2nd Lt. John Norwood. To Norwood's right is Julian Schuck and on the far left his brother, Ed Schuck. Ed's wife was related to the Sultan. The brothers had been educated in Germany. Ed could speak, read and write English, Spanish, Tausug and Samal. He ran a saloon and owned property in Jolo. The Schuck family operated a 1,000 acre coffee plantation on the island. (Photo courtesy of Robert A. Fulton. Used by permission.)

BACK HOME WITH SOUVENIRS

The longer Jack Dowling stayed away, the more he loved and missed his home and family in Renville, Minnesota. Especially Jennie and his "blessed little baby Dorothy" who was then only a year and a half old. When he finally did return, it took four people to carry his luggage off the train. Among the gifts and souvenirs he brought home were a lovely, hand woven cashmere shawl, dainty handkerchiefs made of rare pina cloth (from pineapple fiber), Chinese silks, cut shells, coral and pearls, a woven palm, coolie hat for Dorothy, a rather sinister looking "beheading sword" and even a small, white dog named "Toyse." Dorothy did not know him when he returned and couldn't imagine who this man was with the bushy whiskers. But he knew Dorothy! He had carried the dog in a basket all the way from the Philippines, going through quarantine with it, and it was for her. So, she decided she liked him a lot!

PART TWO

*Dowling's Letters
to the
Minneapolis Journal*

★ Reprinted in full ★

M.J. DOWLING'S TRIP TO MANILA

First Impressions of the Bay and City—A Hotel That is a "Fright"—Troops Well Fed and Comfortable—Heat Not so Bad.

Manila, Philippine Islands,
March 23

My account of experiences in the orient will be that of one who has traveled little and to whom everything is comparatively new. To the reader who has traveled much, my story will be amusing, perhaps, but to him who has seen the world through the spectacles of imagination alone, there may be something in it that will instruct.

I left Renville, Minn., on Feb. 1 of this year, and sailed into Manila Bay a la Dewey at 4:30 a.m. one bright moonlight night in March. Of course, I left a call and was on deck to see Corregidor Island, Cavite, the bay and Manila. Manila Bay is some 200 miles in circumference and forty miles broad at its greatest width. It is roughly circular in shape. There are two entrances from the China Sea. I believe Admiral Dewey took the southern one. I took the northern. The northern passage is one mile and the southern passage about one-half mile in width. Corregidor Island, about one mile long, lies east and west, between these passages. There is a lighthouse on the island and also a marine hospital, and the remains of ancient fortification. I should think modern fortifications on the island would make forcible entrance by the combined fleets of the world impossible.

We steamed eastward into the bay, and, glasses in hand, watched the sun rise over the mountains back of Manila and dispel the morning mists that hung heavily along the shoreline. The first welcome sight was the cruiser Brooklyn, swinging at an anchor off Cavite, which gradually came to view. Cavite is low and from the deck of our steamer looked like a second Dismal Swamp. Coming nearer, we could see the wreck of one of the Spanish cruisers and many more vessels of the United States Navy to the southeast of us, and directly ahead the masts and stacks of merchant ships lying at anchor about two miles out from Manila.

We soon came to anchor beside the large merchantmen, and with signals hoisted, waited for quarantine officers and customs officers. While we were waiting I had an excellent opportunity to scan the shoreline to the east to get an idea of what Manila looked like. I could plainly see the mouth of the Pasig River, and to the south of it the walled city of old Manila, with its solid-looking palace and shore batteries. Further to the south I could see Malate and the little old fort that Dewey shelled, and the beach where our troops were landed to storm the city, and in the distance the dome of the Jesuit observatory. North of the Pasig I could see the city proper, with its mass of low buildings, the lighthouse, and here and there tall church spires. In the background were noble mountains, cloud-bedecked and partly hiding the sun that a few hours later convinced us that this is where he does business without regard for the comfort of people born and bred in a temperate zone.

At 9:30 a tug flying a yellow flag came alongside and the quarantine officers boarded to find that we were without sickness of any kind on board, that no one had died on the trip and that we were entitled to a clean bill of health. When they had performed their duty, they mixed with the passengers and told them of the most important things that had happened in the world during the past four weeks. The news was welcomed. They also told us that the bubonic plague was carrying off a few Chinamen in Manila. This was not quite so welcome, but we congratulated ourselves on the fact that frequent baths and attention to ordinary rules of health might keep us from getting the dread disease.

At about noon, the custom officers came on board to inspect our baggage. I had a steamer trunk and two bags, which I unlocked and opened. The inspector looked at them and asked me if I had any revolvers. I said no, whereupon he said something in a foreign tongue to a very sedate looking Chinaman, who immediately pasted a white label on each piece of baggage, and I was informed that I could go ashore with my luggage whenever I wanted to.

By this time, all kinds of small craft from the dugout paddled by an almost naked native to a steam tug operated by Chinamen had gathered about us for the purpose of selling us fruit, shells or to get a chance to take us ashore. I chose the tug and soon four perspiring coolies were taking my things down and I, with many good-byes to fellow passengers, followed them. It cost me $4 "Mex," or $2 gold to be set down at the Hotel de Oriente. We tied up to a stone wall of solid masonry in front of the captain of the port on the Pasig and were hustled into a carriage and rattled over cobblestone streets at a furious rate to an imposing looking structure styled the Hotel de Oriente. I found the office, stowed away to one side of the entrance, and in charge was an easy-going clerk, who insisted on visiting with me. He said he was from Shanghai, China, that he knew John Goodnow, and that Goodnow was well liked and he was the best consul that ever stirred up Shanghai. I told him that I thought his judgment sound and that Goodnow used to work for me back in the states.

    This seemed to impress him and I was given a large airy room near the baths, a Filipino boy was assigned to me to act as bedroom boy and another to act as bath boy. I was told that the dining room was up two flights of stairs and that I would have to settle my bill once a week at the rate of $7.50 per day. The floor of my room is narra wood, a wood superior to black walnut, the ceiling is painted tin and the walls are of common boards and weather strips both running up and down, all painted blue with some attempt at decoration. The window is eight feet wide and extends from the floor upward about ten feet. It is provided with sliding shutters of wood and sliding doors of glass and outside of these are fancy iron bars to keep any one from getting in to rob one. There is a hall tree for hats, a clothes press, dilapidated wash stand, an ancient looking glass, four cane-seated chairs, a marble top round table and the bed. This bed is a novelty. It looks like the one George Washington died in. You have probably seen it at Mount Vernon. A stepladder is required to get into it. Its four posts run up about nine feet and support a canopy. It is grotesquely carved and a lace curtain hangs down half way and extends all around it. It has a cane bottom as a mattress consisting of one thickness of Japanese matting, on this mattress is a sheet. The pillow for your head extends clear across the bed. Another luxury, and one entirely new to me, is a pillow for your feet. Of course, it is unnecessary for me to say that this is useless to me. Jack Taylor, special correspondent for the Boston Globe, calls it a Dutch wife. Last, but not least, is the mosquito netting. This is ample and runs on two overhead trolleys and must be tucked in under the mattress all around and even then I have found it difficult to leave all the mosquitoes outside when I go to bed.

    The dining room is on the third floor. It is large and airy. Overhead fans of great size are worked by a boy in about the same manner that is employed in furnishing wind for a pipe organ. Chinamen act as waiters and cooks. The meals are not equal to the rankest boarding house hash to be found in Minneapolis. The butter is simply impossible, the milk is condensed and comes from Norway in cans. The coffee is worse than sailors drink. The meats are tough and stringy. The vegetables are palatable. Between the odors and the tastes one is nearly disgusted in an effort to find something fit to eat.

The baths are liberally supplied with cold water and offer the only opportunity of getting one's money's worth from the management. The tubs are of iron and remind one of the old-fashioned soap kettles in which the western pioneers used to manufacture soft soap in "the new of the moon." And yet this is Manila's only first class hotel. Here is a great opening for an American with capital. A real good hotel and bar would be a gold mine for its owner.

The only people here who are well fed are the American troops. The government is really giving its Army first class food and plenty of it, and all that I have seen goes to prove that Uncle Sam will stop at no expense to provide for the common soldier in the Philippines. His meats are brought from the states and Australia in refrigerator ships, his hams and bacons are pure and sweet and his canned goods are fine. The troops show the effect of this treatment. They look robust and healthy. The men's quarters are in the best buildings situated in the best and most healthful parts of the city. The officers have fine quarters and live well. A captain, who formerly served in the British Army in Africa, told me yesterday that he was located up in Luzon with his company, and that he had a fine house to live in; better food than had ever been seen in the British Army, even in times of peace; that his pay as captain was equal to the pay of a major in the British Army, and that if it wasn't for being entirely out of the world, he would want nothing better for the rest of his life.

From what I have seen and heard from both officers and privates, I would advise people at home to take with a grain of salt stories of hardships and dangers sent home by would-be heroes who are looking for sympathy when they picture the trials and tribulations that they are supposed to be enduring here.

This is now the hottest season of the year, the climax being reached about the last of April, and yet I say to you in all seriousness that I have suffered more from the heat in Chicago and New York than I have here, and I am out from 7 o'clock in the morning until 6 or 7 at night without a midday nap and industriously seeking information. I wear two artificial legs and an artificial arm, the harness of which is heavy and lacking in every essential a tendency toward coolness of attire. Yet I have walked in the sun from

1 o'clock in the afternoon until 5, and found it no harder than doing the same thing in Minneapolis in August. I do not mean to say it is not hot. It is hot, but conditions have been exaggerated by over zealous seekers after fame until I think most of the people in the states think as I thought that it would be dangerous to go outside in the middle of the day.

All business houses, including the post office, and excepting the saloons, close at 12:30 p.m. and open again at 2 p.m. The natives and old residents take their siesta at this time. The small shops, the laborers, the Chinese coolies, the cab drivers and the Americans keep on hustling.

The first walk one takes in Manila is apt to be confusing. There is a perfect babel of tongues. The streets are crowded with vehicles of all kinds. The sidewalks are narrow and tip toward the street, which is paved with stones. The stores, except on the Escolta, which is the principal business street, are nothing but booths or holes in the wall. There are three kinds of two-wheeled vehicles here, a sort of jumper, a gig and an Irish jaunting car. The four-wheeled carriages are comfortable to ride in and can be had for 50 cents an hour, that is to say, 25 cents gold, the two-wheeled for 40 cents an hour. With such a cheap method of transportation nearly everybody rides. These carriages are drawn by very strong swift little ponies, a trifle larger than Shetlands. There are also many fine private rigs that can be seen to best advantage any evening on the Luneta, the fashionable and, in fact, the only, drive that approaches an American boulevard. There is a bandstand at one end of this boulevard, which skirts the beach, and every evening a military band discourses music to the assembled multitudes who are out for the fine sea breeze. Last Sunday evening I enjoyed listening to the Sixth Artillery band. The last number on the program was "The Star-Spangled Banner," during the rendering of which every American uncovered and putting to shame many Americans at home. The Filipino coachmen took off their hats.

Standing on the Bridge of Spain, one sees strange sights in the dirty Pasig River. The river is crowded with shipping, the most interesting of which are the dugouts and cascoes. The dugout is a canoe hollowed out of an immense log and capable of floating an immense cargo. It is propelled by natives with paddles of all manner of shapes. The casco is a sort of an Erie canal boat, having a bamboo cabin at either end and outriggers or platforms of bamboo at water-line, along which the native walks as he poles the craft with his long bamboo pole stuck in the mud at the bottom of the river. Whole families live and die in these houseboats. On one I saw a man come out to take a bath and take off his trousers and wash them, putting them back on while his wife was washing rice for dinner about four feet further down stream.

There are very few good buildings in Manila outside of the churches. The vast majority of homes are nipa huts with bamboo floors, about five feet above the ground. One can see the city thoroughly in ten days, although its population exceeds that of San Francisco.

The people, though, offer a great opportunity for study, and in my letters to follow I will endeavor to give the reader my impressions of them.

-M.J. Dowling

WHAT THEY DO IN MANILA

Michael J. Dowling's Second Letter on Filipino Industries and Life, a Most Interesting One.

Manila, P.I., March 28, 1900—This town is so full of interesting things that it is easier to explore than to sit down and write about what you have seen. I find that the native population is decreasing and has been decreasing since 1896 owing largely to the trouble that began in that year with the execution of Dr. Jose Rizal (to whom I will devote a letter as soon as I gather up a few missing details of his romantic life) and has continued to the beginning of the present year.

What do the natives find to do under present circumstances? Why they are fast resuming their former employments and in addition thereto have remunerative positions in the employ of the United States Government and also under American civilians whose wants have greatly increased under the impetus of cheap labor and a hot climate.

A host of them are coachmen, bedroom boys, cooks, waiters, footmen, clerks, office boys and messengers. I find among them, and diligently employing their time, tinsmiths, plumbers, blacksmiths, hat makers, tailors, wood carvers, piano makers, coopers, lumberjacks, butchers, cigar makers, printers, painters, artists, engineers, firemen, pilots and almost every trade and profession usually found in a city of this size.

They imitate almost anything and are artists rather than scientists. They lack the initiative if not the referendum. In short, they require an overseer in most instances.

Who would expect to find a piano factory in Manila? I was very much surprised to discover one the other day at 84 Calle Alcala, district of Santa Cruz, owned and operated by a Filipino, Sr. Dn. Pio Trinidad. He employs quite a number of workmen, all Filipinos and turns out very fine pianos both in sounding qualities and in wood finishing. He exhibited one that was just finished to order for $1,000 Mexican and it was one of the finest finished pianos that I have seen. It is all native wood hand polished and proof against the ravages of the Aug, a worm that ruins every piano of foreign make inside of two years. Sr. Trinidad showed me a Steinway that was brought to him to be recased. I could push my thumb through the wood anywhere. Americans coming here need not bring along a piano. It is better and cheaper to buy one here of native manufacture.

Speaking of pianos reminded me of the fact that the natives use no machinery from the time a tree is felled until it is turned out as a piano, a screen, a piece of furniture or what not and how they accomplish what they do is little short of miraculous. An enterprising Yankee brought over a lot of crosscut saws from San Francisco only to find, when too late, that they would not make a dent in the hard native timber that is sawed with a long, narrow crosscut saw with very fine teeth. There are six kinds of wood here that are equal if not in many ways superior to black walnut and mahogany.

I predict that one of the great industries of these islands will be preparing native woods for export to the United States.

Printers are numerous and earn very little. The three American dailies here employ them to set up all their matter, but the job of proof-reader beggars description. Proofs have to be read and corrected as often as five times on account of the typesetters not knowing anything about the language in which they work.

Of course, the greatest manufacturing interest in the islands is cigar and cigarette making. These cigar factories are very large. They are larger and finer than those at Tampa, FL. I was guided through the "La Insular" concern today and found a large three-story building with very high ceiling and occupying a whole block next to the Bonondo Church. There are over two thousand people employed by this company in this building. They are mostly women and children, although men are employed to make the finest brands. Machinery is used in the manufacture of cigarettes very largely and also in making the cigar boxes. Most of the machinery is of French make, though some is English. The cigarette paper comes in rolls from Paris. I did not see one thing in use made in the United States. The superintendent of the factory is a Scotchman named John D. MacGavin. I asked him a great many questions, of course, and learned among other things that the factory has never lacked tobacco on account of its large warehouses, but that help has been scarce and scared ever since the insurrection began until now. He says he is unable to supply the demand and yet one would think, after visiting the factory, that there were not enough people living to keep this factory going. Mr. MacGavin has lived here twenty-seven years without being away more than twice, once to Hong Kong for a month and once to Europe for nine months. He is a great, big, fleshy Scot whose own word I have for it that he "can drink his whiskey with anybody." This horrible example of what this climate does for a man should be noted with care. I said:

"Mr. MacGavin, we are told in the United States that an American cannot live in the Philippines over two years without endangering his health; are you an exception to the rule laid down for white men?"

He replied: "It's all rot. I tell you this climate is fine; there is no such thing as a cold, catarrh or any similar ailment, and a man can live here as long or longer than he can in any other part of the world if he will simply not try to do too much and be contented."

The longer I stay here and the more I see these natives, the better I like them. I have seen just one person crying since I came. They are a happy lot and are much given to amusement. There are several fine theaters here. Of course, I do not mean as fine as we have in the States, but in comparison with those of the Orient from Bombay to Yokahama. I have the word of W.H. Brown, of England, who has been an advance agent for shows in these parts for seven years, that Manila has the largest and finest theater in the Orient. The best one will seat 1,500 and is well built. Native plays are staged and well patronized.

The native stores are managed by the women. In fact, most of the matters financial are managed by the gentler sex. They appear to have more of an eye to business than do their pleasure-loving husbands. The Chinese keep these female merchants on the jump to get trade. In fact, the Chinese are too much for them. The natives hold their own in the sale of Pina cloth because it is of their own manufacture. It is a delicate cloth, that looks to be a cross between linen and silk, and is made from pineapple fiber. Just now it is scarce and sells at from $1 to $2.50 per yard of 33 inches. The best grade comes from Caloocan. Every visitor to the Philippines wants some of it, because it is distinctively Filipino. A Filipino dude always wears white cotton trousers, a pina shirt, with the tails outside the trousers, a palm hat, white shoes and under one arm a game cock, in the other hand a cigarette. He is, like his prototype in the states, a gentleman of leisure or a boy who spends all his earnings in buying clothes.

In the matter of morals, it seems to be generally conceded that the men are, as a rule, liars and thieves, while the women lack virtue. I have found neither to be true; but I grant that I have not been here very long. I have poked around into all parts of the city, and while brevity of dress is common, the women are modest, and, so far as I have been able to learn, virtuous. This is a tropical climate, and hence these people deserve great credit for whatever virtues they possess. The only women who openly and boldly solicit immoral patronage are white women, and there are a great many of them here to help civilize the natives by their example. One house of ill-fame is not a stone's throw from a public school for girls. Comment is unnecessary. I am afraid that if the native women judge American women by the kind they see in these places, the idea that we are uncivilized will gain lodgement in their minds.

Military rule should give way to a civil administration of this city at least, and an example of just administration shown the natives. This would help materially in future dealings with natives.

Ten years of American rule will work wonders here provided we are careful and conscientious in our work. The opportunity is ours and we should make the most of it. The natives will, in that time, surprise the world with their progress. They need above all things just treatment in order that ambition may prosper on the field of employment.

Up in the mountains of Colorado, some years ago, there was an Irishman chopping pine trees into cordwood at $1 per cord. He was working for a man who was considered "poor pay," and somehow it was noticed that this Irishman never chopped more than one cord a day. Asked why he didn't chop more, the Irishman replied to the gentleman asking the question, who, by the way needed a good man and was "good pay," that "you see, sir, it is this way, the man I am working for charges me $1 a day for board, and while I could chop four or five cords a day, I don't see any need of doing it when there is no show of getting any more than my board out of it, so I chop just enough to keep out of debt while I am waiting for a job that will pay."

These natives are a great deal like that Irishman. They have for generations been working for the Spaniards for their board. If they made more, it was taken away from them somehow. This discouraged them, and they finally let go of ambition and took to amusement, working enough to pay their taxes and buy their food and thereby keep out of jail and the poor house. Now, if Uncle Sam will let them understand that they can get just as rich as it is possible for them to do and that the government will protect them in the possession of their riches, I believe they will go to work, get ambitious and before many years fit themselves for the competitions of life, and thereby learn the reasonableness of government and be able to administer their own affairs wisely and well.

-M.J. Dowling

MANY CHANCES IN MANILA

M.J. Dowling in His Third Letter Points Out How Fortunes May Be Made in the Philippine Capital

Manila, P.I., March 31—As stated in a previous letter, most of the merchants here are not Filipinos. The largest concerns here represent English, German, Spanish and Chinese capital. The United States is as yet poorly represented except in saloons, restaurants and kindred concerns. Nearly all business is confined to the forenoon, the stores closing at 12:30 and opening again at 2 pm and remaining open until 5:30, when carriages are usually secured and a drive on the Luneta to the music of a band is indulged in until 7 o'clock. Late dinners are fashionable. The dinner hour is seldom earlier than 7:30 pm and extends to 9:30 pm. In spite of these hours a great deal of business is done and profits are enormous. Many men have made fortunes here inside of five years and it is confidently predicted that, with free trade here and the same opportunities guaranteed in Chinese ports, vast fortunes will be gathered in by the men of capital who get on the ground and go in with the tide.

From eight to twenty ships arrive here every day and this is not counting United States army boats. There are not enough cascoes, lighters, bancas or steam launches to handle the freight and passengers who pass through the port of Manila. Here is a chance for someone to devise more modern ways of handling freight. Really the government should have a modern coaling station here and not be compelled to depend upon a line of Chinese passing coal up in little baskets from cascoes as is done at present. Then, too, it would appear, to a land lubber like me, that a channel like the jetties at New Orleans would be feasible and practicable here at the mouth of the Pasig. If large ships could come up the river to docks instead of anchoring two miles out, much time and expense would be saved, enough, I should think, to pay the cost of the improvement in a few years.

The United States has in contemplation the building of two or three more bridges across the Pasig and they are certainly needed. The bridges now existing are crowded to their utmost capacity and are poor excuses at that.

The Escolta is the principal business street. It is always congested and is entirely inadequate to the demand for room made upon it. When the new bridges are built and when American capital wakes up to its opportunity, the business center will move up the river to the Quiapo and Santa Cruz districts where streets are wider and where the sidewalks are more than mere hat brims. When that happy day comes let us hope it will witness the departure of the slow-going and obstructive carabao and his creaking cart, as well as the miserable excuse for a street railway. Tom Lowry would find a good investment here and be hailed as a benefactor of mankind. An electric street railway with extensions along the beach and back to the mountains offers capital an opportunity that should not go begging many months.

The telephone system is European and consequently not an up-to-date American institution. In order to do any telephoning one has to talk at a board and use both hands to hold two receivers, one at each ear. This makes it very unsatisfactory for men with one arm.

The only really good semi-public convenience is the electric light plant.

Manila will soon be on the tourists' list of visiting places and this will provide handsome opportunities for bright young Americans to act as guides. If someone wants to make money let him come here and organize an A.D.T. and provide intelligent guides for sightseers.

A good bakery would pay and so would a good clean American produce market.

A dairy is sadly needed, and would bring big profits in the sale of fresh milk. Butter would sell at fabulous prices. Of course stock would have to be imported. I am inclined to think that arrangements could be made with the government by which transportation would be cheapened. Cows do well in the West Indies and, therefore, ought to thrive here, especially the Jersey breed.

With a fine beach close to the business and resident sections of the town, yet there are no opportunities for bathing. An American who would come here and establish a bathhouse pavilion and have steam launches and rowboats for hire would certainly get good returns from his investment. The people love pleasure, and everything in that line is sure to be a success.

An American hotel would be a fine investment. It need not necessarily be built on expensive ground. If such an institution existed, people would be willing to go to the suburbs to patronize it. The present accommodations in this respect are simply unbearable. Such a hotel as one generally finds in most watering places in America would be filled with guests who would willingly pay $5 gold per day and even more. A good bar, laundry, livery, guides and messengers in connection would coin money.

An American bank is also needed. There are three large banks here at present. All are doing a very large business. The rates of exchange with the United States are almost prohibitive. To get a $1,000 draft cashed, one is compelled to pay $40 Mexican–more than is required in Hong Kong. Americans generally patronize the post office, and yet the postmasters of the United States do not seem to understand that they can sell post office money orders on Manila. Why an American bank has not been established before this is past comprehension.

If capitalists of America are looking for profitable investments, let them turn their attention to the Philippines and especially to Manila. The Pacific coast states will profit immeasurably: from this trade and the great northwest should not permit other sections of the country or other nations to gather up these splendid opportunities. I have not seen a single sack or barrel of Minneapolis flour here although large quantities are used and could be exchanged to advantage for native products.

Young men can find something to do if made of the right kind of stuff. I know a young American here who is only 23 years of age. He is making thousands and thousands of dollars, but he's business with a big B. It costs about $300 to reach Manila from the Mississippi River and one should bring along a return ticket and have enough to live on a few months while investigating conditions. Two weeks in Manila will give anyone a fair idea of business conditions and opportunities, though a longer period is required to thoroughly overhaul all lines.

In closing this letter I would advise men of small means to keep away from here as yet, but to men with capital I unhesitatingly say come, a harvest awaits you.

-M.J. Dowling

MANUFACTURING IN MANILA

M.J. Dowling's Fourth Letter Describes Interestingly the Small Factories and Their Products

Manila, P.I., April 2, 1900—Sunday in Manila under military rule differs little from any other day in the week. Of course, military operations cannot be suspended on Sunday, and the Chinese population, seeing the Americans carrying on operations, keep their stores open. The natives quite generally close their shops, after attending church, go to cockfights or attend the races at the Manila Country Club or otherwise make a gala day of it.

Yesterday, being Sunday, I went with the crowd to the grounds of the country club and for three hours enjoyed the races and the crowd of betting natives and Chinese. This club is operated by Americans, several of whom are Army and Navy officers. Like everything else here, the track is odd, being three-fourths of a mile around and the horses run the opposite way to what they do in the states. Even the pools are sold wrong end to. I saw some very hotly contested races. The first race (running) was for a purse of $250 Mex., distance three-quarters of a mile. It was won by a little bay pony fifty inches high and carrying 122 pounds in 1:40-1/4. In the second race, an American horse ridden by a major in the regular Army, won over two Australian horses, making his half mile in :55-3/4. The longest distance run in any of the races, was one and one-fourth miles. A native pony made it in 2:64. As usual in such places, the last race was the best one in the bunch and put everybody in the proper mood to insure their attendance on the following Sunday.

The visitor to Manila should not miss the races. The grounds are located outside of the city and the grandstand, with its bamboo chairs and bamboo floors, is commodious and comfortable. Gentle sea breezes fan the excited mass of people, and the seductive seller of pools relieves you of an overplus of Mexican silver.

After the races, I drove for an hour on the Luneta and listened to the excellent music of a regimental band. This is the one great pleasure of all the residents of Manila who are rich enough to own a carriage or who feel equal to the expenditure of 50 cents Mex. for a carametta. On this beautiful evening of the first day in April the Luneta was crowded to its utmost capacity and the guards were kept busy straightening out the mix-ups. A new moon looked down on the gay throng and hundreds of ships' lights from the placid bay lent charm to the scene. The walls of the old city, with its mounted cannon, and the lights of the new city in the background, only needed the gentle fanning sea breeze to make one think he was on enchanted ground. The breeze was there, and the balmy atmosphere was there, and when the band played "The Star-Spangled Banner" we realized that Uncle Sam was there, and off came all hats, while many a thought was telegraphed across more than six thousand miles of sea to the folks at home.

Today I diligently employed my time visiting the tiny factories of the natives and Chinese and found much to wonder at, as well as much to admire. It seemed like being taken back through the centuries to a time when everything was done by hand and when it was necessary for everyone to be employed to furnish common needs. I found them cutting up discarded cans from the quartermaster's department and making tin cups, plates and lamps from them. In one shop, the occupants were grinding chocolate beans and peanuts together, showing that adulteration is not confined to the United States. In another they were making soap and cutting it into small cakes with a piece of wire or cutting out round cakes with a punch. Another contained a jolly crowd making slippers which they were anxious to sell for sixty cents Mex. per pair. In these shops, I noticed many sewing machines run by hand. They are of American manufacture and cost the natives $25 Mex. They are usually paid for on the installment plan. Many of these machines are also found in the tailor shops, which are very numerous. The general agent for this sewing machine company tells me that the insurrection has done him a great deal of damage on account of the number of natives who have seized the opportunity to leave the city without paying the balance due on machines in their possession. He says it is all cash now or no machine. Since this rule went into effect, sales have diminished.

In one factory, natives were making rope by hand. In another, baskets and cases were being woven by hand out of bamboo. In others, they were making boxes to take the place of trunks, which they sell to soldiers returning to the states. Still others were making candy, refined sugar, bamboo hats, canes, pipes, and medicines from herbs and roots; but the most interesting one I found was an oil mill. This oil mill is located at No. 37 Calle Santo Cristo and has been in operation thirty years. It gives employment to three Chinese and one Chino-Mestizo. The oil is such a perfect counterpart of linseed oil that I could not distinguish any difference either in appearance or odor. It is used to mix with other ingredients to form paint. There were four of these mills in Manila before the American occupation. The demand for paint since then has caused the creation of two additional mills. There is one other province in the Philippines where there are other oil mills, but the number is not large. The oil is made from the meat of the seed of the fruit of the Lumbang tree. The tree is said to exist only in the Philippine and Caroline Islands. The tree grows to great size in Laguna province, about forty miles from Manila. The fruit looks like an apple, but it is not edible. The kernel of the seed is secured and packed in gunny sacks, which, filled, weigh a pico, or 137-1/2 pounds, and cost, laid down in Manila, $6.75 Mex. The crusher used is a large conical granite stone with a hole through the center. In this hole is a pole about six inches in diameter extending from a pivot in the center of the ring to a track outside, where a blindfolded water buffalo is hitched to it and patiently drags it around, causing the stone to roll over and crush the mass of nut kernels in its path. When thoroughly crushed, the mass is scooped up and put into a press made out of a log split into halves, which are forced together by a windlass arrangement worked by hand by means of wooden levers. This pressure is very effective and the oil is forced out into a catch basin and thence transferred to vats for sale. The waste or solid substance remaining is made into dry pieces about the shape and size of a candy pail cover and sold for palayad or fertilizer to farmers, who use it in growing the leaves which are used to wrap up betel nuts that are so commonly chewed by all the inhabitants of the islands. This palayad, or, as the Spaniards call it, abono, sells at $12.50 per hundred pieces. The oil is called oil of lumbang, and a measure holding six pounds sells for 72 cents Mex. My judgment is that this measure holds about one-half gallon of oil. The capacity of this mill is about 500 pounds of oil per day. At this rate it ought to pay American capital to import linseed oil or perhaps establish a modern mill for the manufacture of oil of lumbang. The supply of lumbang is unlimited in the Philippines and if necessary the Carolines can be drawn on, although the 20 days' sail has a tendency to dry the nuts and thereby lower the grade of the product. This is only one of the many openings for American capital. In another letter, I will endeavor to describe a native flouring or grist mill and a coconut oil mill. On the 4th inst I will sail on the Pennsylvania for a complete tour of the islands, after having spent nearly a month in the city of Manila. The tour will take six weeks or two months, during which time I will send letters whenever possible.

-M.J. Dowling

DOWLING'S VISIT TO ILOILO

A Careful Study of the Canteen—The Wonderful Church at Molo—Work of the Sisters

V.

Correspondence of The Journal.

Iloilo, P.I., Good Friday, April 13, 1900.—After seven days in this port, I expect to sail before noon for Cebu. We left Manila on the afternoon of April 4 and passed the light on Corregidor Island at about 9 o'clock in the evening. We awoke next morning in San Bernardino Strait, skirting the eastern shore of the Island of Mindoro and in plain sight of an active volcano. To the east of us, through our glasses, we could see Marinduque Island. All day long, the Island of Mindoro lay to the westward of us, presenting an ever-changing panorama of view that kept the glasses constantly to the eyes. In the afternoon, we could see Tablas Island to the eastward, and before sunset we passed Point Nasog, which is the northwestern point of the Island of Panay. Early the morning of April 6, we rounded Naso Point, which is the southwestern point of Panay. By 7 o'clock we were steaming rapidly up Guimaras Strait in the midst of some of the most beautiful scenery that I have looked upon. To the southward were bluffs, for all the world like the Hudson Highlands. They were the hills of the Island of Guimaras, which lies opposite the city of Iloilo. Little glens peeped out here and there from among the rugged bluffs of the island, where native huts, protected by towering coconut palms, lay sheltered from the fierce, searching rays of the sun. To the northward, on the Island of Panay, were miles of coconut trees and in the shallow water were corrals or fish pounds with numerous small sailing craft dotting the water. These fishing pounds are very interesting. They are especially adapted to a people who are too lazy to fish with a pole and line or with a net. A place is selected where during low tide the water is not more than one foot deep, or perhaps where no water stands at all. The natives drive long bamboo poles into the ground to a depth of maybe ten feet, leaving about six feet protruding above the ground. The shape of the yard or pound is usually square with posts close together. Strips of bamboo are then taken and woven into a mat fence. This fence is so closely woven that nothing but water can leak out. Two gates are then made, one on the shore side, the other opposite. When constructed this pound is closed tightly and old ocean does the rest; that is to say, high tide comes in and covers up the entire pound. The fish naturally swim back and forth through the water, and coming to this closely woven fence, rise to the top, go over and drop to the bottom again, where they feed. In this manner they pass freely in and out, but when the tide ebbs, many fish find themselves imprisoned and an easy prey to the watchful native owner of the pound.

Hot at Iloilo

We arrived at Iloilo at 8:30 a.m. Friday, April 6, and I went ashore to spend the day. It was the hottest day that I have ever experienced, although the thermometer didn't register above 97 degrees in the shade. I spent the day roaming around in the dust of the streets, visiting the shops, warehouses at the docks, the old fort and other points of interest. I was told at the weather station, which is maintained by representatives of the Catholic Church in an old cathedral, that this was the hottest day in fifty years. As soon as I found this out, I repaired to a soft drink establishment and poured down glass after glass of lemon soda. My face was as red as a boiled lobster and the perspiration rolled off me in streams until I was as wet as though I had been ducked in a mill pond. During the week that I was in Iloilo, I drove to the neighboring villages of Molo and Jaro, visiting the people in their homes and on their farms. I also sailed on the Strait of Guimaras, narrowly escaping a tipover. I visited the Island of Guimaras, which is said to be the most healthful of the Philippines. The soil is on limestone rock and fevers are unknown. Drainage is perfect and the landscape is a dream of delight. Natives are busy. They ferry all they raise and manufacture in their bancoes to Iloilo. The Strait at this point, by the way, is between five and six miles in width, with anchorage for the largest man-of-war. Iloilo, except that portion of it situated on a sandy point terminating in an old fort, is desolate looking now because of the great fire set by the insurgents before our occupation. General Hughes, who is in command of our troops, is rapidly rebuilding the town, which is said to be second only to Manila in commercial importance in the Philippines.

The Army Canteen

One interesting feature of Iloilo is the fact that it contains no saloons. There is not a saloon on the Island of Panay. The sale of liquor is limited to the Army canteen and as this is the first opportunity I have had of witnessing the

Army canteen in operation where there were no saloons, I became very much interested in finding out all about it. I found that before a private soldier or civilian could get a drink of beer or whiskey, he would have to go in person to the provost marshal and procure a permit. This permit is a printed slip in the blank spaces of which the officer—in this instance the son of a New York millionaire—writes your name and the amount and kind of liquor that you are thereby entitled to purchase. I was told that privates are seldom granted permission to purchase whiskey. Privates are required to drink their beer on the premises, thereby shutting off the possibility of some comrade purchasing beer for a soldier whose appetite for liquor is so well known to the provost marshal that he is unable to get a permit for the purchase of the stuff for himself. The canteen is not popular with a number of Americans here who would like to go into the saloon business. They abuse the system and declare that the United States Government has no right to refuse its citizens license to do business. One man told me that the canteen would have to go. I asked him how this would be accomplished. He said the religious people of the United States would work upon the sentiment of the people against the canteen, while large brewing and distilling corporations would look after congress, and between the two something was bound to come. This struck me as rather a peculiar partnership. The idea of hitching up religious corporations with the brewers and distillers! I cannot believe that the church people of the United States will be led into this trap. I can see why the brewers and distillers would prefer the saloon to the canteen. They would, of course, sell more liquor. It is apparent to everybody with even limited worldly experience that liquor will be manufactured and sold and I cannot help thinking that our church people at home would prefer the well regulated Army canteen to the grog shop. Take it in Manila where saloons are numerous—drunken soldiers are common. Beer and whiskey are both consumed to excess. Disease follows, hospitals are crowded and commands crippled. Here in Iloilo I have not seen a drunken man during the whole week I have been here. The soldiers look rugged, the one hospital is comparatively empty. The men are nearly all from Massachusetts, where saloons, inns and roadhouses are numerous and where the working people are by no means total abstainers. The health of the troops, as stated before, is excellent in spite of the fact that Iloilo is built on low, marshy ground, where the sun's rays are as fierce as, if not fiercer, than in Manila. Inquiry developed another interesting fact. The troops stationed at Iloilo have more money on deposit with the paymaster than any of those in the saloon districts of Manila have. The profits of the canteen go into the company or regimental fund, the money being used to buy delicacies for the convalescent sick and books and magazines for the well. It should not be overlooked either that the liquor in the Army canteen is as pure as can be purchased, while that in saloons may or may not be, according to the character of the saloon-keeper. Pure liquors are bad, adulterated liquors are worse. From what I have seen in Manila and in Iloilo, I am unqualifiedly in favor of the Army canteen as against the saloon. It may be interesting to state in this connection that swearing, loud talking and boisterous conduct are absolutely prohibited in and about the canteen. Instead of card playing gambling, obscene story telling and kindred pastimes usually found in a saloon, the canteen furnishes good reading matter and prohibits gambling. Before the church and the breweries form their partnership, I would suggest that our churchmen think this over a little. The older we grow, the more apparent it becomes to every one of us that it is necessary at times to make a choice between evils, because we have learned that we cannot mold this old world of ours into shapes that will agree with our ideals of integrity and morality. My observations, of course, would have no effect upon a radical prohibitionist, but experience in the states teaches that there is a large element composed of honest citizens which believes in taking a sensible course that lies somewhere between radical prohibition and the wide open policy of those who live on the diseased appetites of their fellows.

The Church at Molo

One of the most interesting villages on the Island of Panay is Molo. I engaged a guide, hired a carriage and drove out there early one morning and remained until 5 o'clock in the afternoon. It is about five and a half miles from Iloilo over a dilapidated turnpike, on both sides of which are native huts crowded with people who cultivate the soil for rice.

The most interesting building in Molo is the magnificent Catholic Church, which is as large as any of the cathedrals that I have seen in the United States. Its interior impresses one with awe. The floor is of stone; great pillars rise to a height of, I should judge, forty feet, supporting the beautifully decorated ceiling. The walls as well as the ceilings have been painted by some of the best artists of Europe and represent scenes in the life of Christ from His birth to His crucifixion. Prayer stations and confessionals are numerous.

A great gallery over the entrance affords ample space for a huge choir. The ground plan of the church resembles a great cross, at the head and arms of which are altars—five in number. Carriages covered with candelabra are stationed near these altars and can be moved about the interior at will. Huge candlesticks of solid silver, with golden ornaments, are used in profusion in the decoration of the altars, while golden censers on wheels and movable founts of holy water stood ready to be moved throughout the length and breadth of this magnificent building, wherein there is neither pew nor chair, the floor being entirely free from any obstruction except the great pillars. I find that I am unable to adequately describe the interior of this fine structure, which is said to be not only the finest in the Philippines, but equal to some of the best in the world in its decorations and furnishings. One doesn't need to be a Catholic to have his sense of admiration deeply stirred after viewing the interior of this church. No one can view it without commending the religious zeal of the churchmen who built it. It is a monument to that great something in the Catholic Church which has caused her priests to penetrate the wildest parts of the earth for the purpose of spreading Catholicism.

Who Stole the Image?

Since Magellan was laid away to rest on the Island Mactan, the natives of the Philippines have made a long stride in civilization, for which the friars, and even Spain, deserve a measure, however small, of our commendation. I will address myself to the subject of the friars when observation shall have equipped me to speak with knowledge.

Father Miguel, a native friar at Molo, entertained me at his house and gave me much valuable information. I had heard the story of how the Tennessee troops had robbed the church, and took this occasion to ask Father Miguel as to the truth of this statement. He said that in the church above described there had been a golden image twelve inches high, studded with diamonds and other precious stones and valued at $3,000. Some time during the occupation of Molo by the Tennessee troops this image was stolen. He did not say that the troops stole it. The loss was reported to the commanding officer of the American troops, who immediately ordered a thorough search of every soldier and every piece of baggage in the camp, without finding the image. He volunteered the further information that nothing else had been defaced, destroyed or stolen since the American occupation of the island.

The Work of the Sisters

I made two unsuccessful attempts to visit the sisters at their convent at Molo. As far as I got on either occasion was the foot of the stairs, where I had an opportunity to look over the carriages and ponies that were stored and stabled on the ground floor of the convent. These carriages were of excellent workmanship and did not show very much wear and tear. I had heard much about the fine needlework of the sisters and felt very much disappointed upon being politely refused an audience. However, I visited the family living in the adjoining house, where I found four looms in operation manufacturing jusi cloth. I secured samples of the hemp, cotton and silk threads on bamboo bobbins. The old looms resemble the Irish linen loom and look as though they might fall to pieces at the least touch. The spinning wheels also look dilapidated. The women of the house brought out their bolts of cloth for my inspection and placed their figures high enough for my supposed wealthy condition. I showed a disposition to go away without buying anything, whereupon I was tendered a vile looking cigar and a glass of vino. I accepted the cigar, which proved to be better than it looked, and turned the vino over to my guide and interpreter. This vino, by the way, is dangerous stuff for an American to drink, as it makes one insanely intoxicated. The natives don't patronize our canteens or saloons, but it would be a great deal better for them if they would, rather than that they should continue to drink vino, which is the fermented juice of coconut buds. While enjoying the cigar, I told the Filipino women that I would like to buy some pina handkerchiefs nicely worked. They said they didn't have any but that the sisters had some next door and they would go over and get some samples to show me. When brought and laid before me, they proved to be marvelous specimens of needlework. One handkerchief of pina drawn work with some hand painting on it and the name of the sisters' convent worked in silk was offered to me for $60. It is needless to say, that I got even with my good sisters by shopping without purchasing any of their needlework.

Iloilo, Molo and Jaro are the center of the jusi manufacturing district of the islands. Some enterprising Americans could come to Iloilo with a few thousand dollars gold and corner the product. I have no doubt but that this dress goods would bring a high figure in the states. The best quality readily sells here at $1 Mexican per yard.

Instead of closing this letter, I would continue column after column telling of the people and industries of this place. I would like to tell you what

I think of the differences between these people—who are Visayans—and the Tagalos of the northern islands, but I will wait until I have studied the Moros of the southern islands.

-M.J. Dowling

M.J. DOWLING LOOKS CEBU OVER CAREFULLY

The Cause of Public Education—Filth of the Houses—Hostility to Americans—A Strong Sentiment in Favor of Bryan's Election

Correspondence of The Journal.

VI

Cebu, P.I., April 17, 1900.—I sailed from Iloilo Friday the 13th. We skirted the north coast of Guimaras to its western extremity, upon which is a lighthouse most beautifully situated among coconut and other palm trees far enough apart to give it the appearance of a natural park. Heading southwest from this point, we passed within sight of Cartagena. During the night we rounded the southern point of Negros Island, passed up the west shore of Sigijor, and during the forenoon of April 14 had beautiful sailing northward, with the Island of Cebu on the west and Bohol on the east, striking in between Cebu and the small island of Mactan, about half past 10 o'clock, and casting anchor close in to the city of Cebu at 11 o'clock.

Before the anchor had fairly touched bottom, our ship was surrounded by bancoes crowded with naked children of both sexes, jawing away at the top of their voices and frantically sawing the air with their arms. Some of the passengers knew what they meant and commenced throwing coppers over for the youngsters to dive after. The fun was fast and furious until all the coppers the crowd possessed had found their way to little niches in the bancoes. The sport was so fascinating that many silver pieces found their way overboard. I remember one diver who was, I should judge, 17 years of age, who made the most magnificent dive I have ever seen. He dived after a Mexican half-dollar and was under water for several minutes, a portion of the time so deep as to be invisible although the water is quite clear. In connection with this diving, one must not forget that the tide here between the Islands of Mactan and Cebu runs like a sluiceway. These bancoes, filled with divers, hung about us for several days. Others came regularly with pineapples, mangoes, coconuts and fine shells, which they offered for sale.

The City of Cebu

The city of Cebu is prettily situated on a point of land on the extremity of which is an old weather-beaten fort that has more than once furnished the Spaniards a place of refuge from the natives. The Island of Cebu is about 150 miles long and from 10 to 35 miles in width. Three distinct ranges of mountains traverse the length of this island. The rivers are necessarily short, the coasts high and the country difficult of access; in fact, it is one of the strongholds of the native insurrectos.

Cebu has an area of about 2,000 square miles with a population of about a half million. A part of this population is composed of savage tribes in the mountains. The city of Cebu is supposed to contain somewhere between 15,000 and 35,000 inhabitants. It is the capitol of the island and 460 miles from Manila. It is the oldest Spanish settlement in the Philippines and its natives were the first converts to Christianity. Before the building of Manila, it was the commercial center of the islands and today it is one of the busiest ports outside of Manila. It is here that Magellan landed and raised the cross and colors of Spain nearly 400 years ago. The oldest church of the islands is shown to the visitors within the walls of the old fort and the cross that Magellan raised is preserved here. Across a narrow strait is the Island of Mactan, where the great explorer was killed by the natives while championing the cause of one of the chieftains of a tribe that inhabited Cebu. The spot where he was killed by the arrow of a native is marked by a shabby looking monument. The Island of Mactan is only eight feet above the sea. It is a coral island. The only town on it is Opon on the west coast, where Magellan was killed in 1521. There is a wagon road on the east coast connecting the capitol with a score of towns. This, together with the waterway, brings a great many people into the city, giving the place the appearance of being a lively market town. As in other towns, there are fine churches and public buildings. One of the most powerful bishops of the archipelago lives here in a fine palace. I saw him go down the street one day holding out his right hand, which the natives crowded around to kiss. They ran eagerly from all directions upon being told that the bishop was passing, and fairly trampled each other under foot in an effort to touch the hem of his garment or kiss his hand.

There is a large cathedral here, a fine convent, a good seminary, a leper hospital and one of the most beautiful cemeteries on the island. Easter Sunday in Cebu was an occasion for great festivities. One feature was a religious procession consisting of floats drawn by natives; upon these floats were arranged the most beautiful and comely of the natives to represent Christ, the Apostles, the Virgin Mary, etc., each float representing one event in the life of Christ from His birth to His crucifixion. As this procession moved slowly through the crowded streets, natives by the thousands literally buried their faces in the dust before it. A good band furnished the music and children's voices formed numerous choirs. It was the Oberammergau "Passion Play" in miniature. These festivities taught me to believe that these natives are very devoted church people, at least they pay most particular attention to the observance of holy days and the rituals of the church. Among the churches of Cebu is that of the Augustines, which is famous because it possesses a miraculous image of the "Santo Ninnyo." I was privileged to view this image, which is placed in a little niche behind locked doors in the rear of and above the altar of the church. The story goes that this image dropped from heaven during an earthquake or storm of some kind centuries ago and was found on the beach—a perfect image of the Christ child. It was solid gold. Those who came to see it were cured of many ills and in gratitude left precious stones, which were used in decorating the image. This continued until the value of the image thus jeweled is said to have been fabulous. About this time, the Pope desired to see it and it was sent to him. After many mishaps, it reached Rome and was blessed. Upon being returned, it was found that another miracle had been performed—nothing but the former shape of the image was left—the material having been changed to a dark wood. I do not vouch for the truth of the above story but simply give what came to me. Whatever the history of the image, the fact remains that as it now stands I would gladly accept it as a gift for its intrinsic value. The holy fathers in charge of this church and its famous image are most excellent entertainers. No Americans need go away without having tasted of famous wines and puffed smoke from aromatic cigars.

Manufactures of Cebu

Rain is scarce in Cebu; so is arable land. However, the city of Cebu is the center of a number of islands which send their products here for export. The trade of this port exceeds 6,000,000 pesos a year. Manufactures consist of soap, silk, pinya cloth, abaca (hemp) and cotton. This cotton grows in pods about five inches long on great trees. I threw a club into the branches of one of these trees and brought down several pods to take home with me as curiosities. Pillows and quilts stuffed with this cotton are offered for sale by native women on the wharf. The most interesting place to me in Cebu is the hemp gin. From the surrounding islands large bancoes and native as well as Spanish sloops and schooners come laden to the gunwales with hemp, or, as the natives call it, abaca. This is dragged ashore through the shallow water by the armful and loaded into bull carts and taken to the great warehouses, where it is sorted according to quality and paid for by the "pickol," which is about 140 pounds. It is then placed in presses, some of which are worked by hand, and at least one by hydraulic pressure, and made into bales something like the cotton bales of the south. Each bale has exactly two pickols in it, and at this time is selling for $22 gold per bale. This hemp, or abaca, so necessary for binding twine in the wheat-raising section of the United States, as well as so indispensable to sailors for cordage, hausers and cables, is grown in great profusion by the natives on stony side-hills and steep declivities. The plant is a species of banana and the fibers are about the size and coarseness of the hairs in a horse's tail and in length about eight feet. Inter-island steamers of light draught are heavily laden with this hemp when baled and taken to Manila, where it is shipped in large sailing vessels and steamers by the thousands of tons to Europe, New York and Boston. The natives are expert in making cloth of these fibers. They also make fine ropes which they use in the rigging of their sailing vessels. I saw one schooner with sails made out of woven hemp. I saw ponies hitched to carriages, and every particle of their harness was made out of hemp, even to the blinds on the bridle. There wasn't a particle of iron or leather in them.

A Plague of Dust

On account of the lack of rain, the dust in Cebu is something terrible. It is no exaggeration to say that the dust in the streets, pulverized by traffic, lies three and four inches deep, and clouds of it follow any movement through it.

One sees some queer carts here, with immovable axles and solid wheels, being nothing more nor less than a section of a log about three inches thick with an iron tire. Rigs for hire are not as numerous as in Manila, neither are charges as reasonable. I find that the people have to import rice, and, while this might be done from neighboring islands, in this instance the foreign dealers get it from Hong Kong and sell it to the natives in exchange for hemp, etc., at the rate of $5.20 a pickol.

With the Troops

A proportion of the Nineteenth Infantry is stationed here under command of Col. E.J. McClernand. They have excellent quarters in a large stone building called a quartel. After several days' wading in the dust, I wanted to go out into the country or sail around the Island of Mactan, but Colonel McClernand warned me not to attempt it, stating that it is not safe to go beyond the outposts, which are stationed about a mile from town. Wherever a few soldiers stray beyond the line, they are promptly killed by the alert natives. Saloons exist here, and two soldiers who had visited them too often for their own good strayed beyond the lines a few days before my arrival and were boloed, being literally cut to pieces.

I have stated in a former letter my belief in the ability of the natives in the larger towns to govern their own municipality under the guidance of the commanding officer of our troops. This is actually being done in Cebu and, strange as it may seem, the form of civil government here is the one promulgated by Aguinaldo.

By invitation of Colonel McClernand I was present at the first meeting between him and the native officers of the civil government of Cebu. They were Timoteo de Castro, city treasurer; Marcial Velez, chief of district; Cirilo Canizares, city doctor, and Renovato Eugenio Cordero, civil government interpreter. There were also present Major Wm. F. Lippett and Captain S.C. Samuels who formed a board in charge of the health of the city. It was amusing to hear the good city fathers say that there wasn't a cent in the city treasury. They wanted the colonel to furnish some, but upon being questioned they said that they could make the rich natives and the Chinese pay some taxes. The colonel instructed them to raise some money, plant trees in the plaza, fill up sink holes, clean the streets, build public toilet conveniences, remove garbage and in every possible way clean the town and keep it clean. This they promised to do and seemed pleased to have the American officers entrust them with the work. They were an intelligent and clean-looking body of men. Through the courtesy of Signor Cordero, I had an opportunity of going with the native officials on a tour of inspection of the city. Such filth I had never seen before. We went through the native huts from one end of the town to the other and that trip beggars description. The native officers looked upon it with complacency, but readily understood my disgust when I pointed to the cesspools of filth that existed right under each and every nipa but, where children, dogs, chickens and hogs moved about with equal freedom and where the stench was something quite unbearable. Strange to say, the families in these huts looked clean and they actually do take baths quite frequently. In nearly every instance we found some of the children sick with fever; smallpox was not uncommon, and yet there are a great many very aged people among them. To get into some of the huts we had to climb a short ladder, the floor of the huts was simply a coarse mat woven from half-inch pieces of bamboo with the convex side up. A hole in the floor was used through which to cast rubbish and refuse of all kinds. Very little attempt at decoration is made in the houses of these people and that only along the line of their faith. There is little attempt at privacy—whole families existing in one room. In many of the poorer huts I could take the whole belongings—furniture, clothing, cooking utensils, etc., under one arm and walk away with it without any inconvenience.

Rice and fish are the principle articles of diet. Many of the poorest of the women, clothed with nothing but a single piece of cloth, had jewels on their fingers that would be the envy of some of our best dressed society women in the United States. The sex here as well as in America loves decoration and is not unmindful of the charms of face and figure. One very noticeable feature is that the women here powder to such an extent as to give one the impression that they belong to the Caucasian race.

The Public Schools

There are five public schools in Cebu, organized and supported by the United States Government. Signor Cordero told me that not one-sixth of the children attended school, and yet these five school buildings are crowded beyond their capacity. A description of one of them will answer for all. I visited Escuela Publica de Ninos de Este Cuidad. Before going upstairs where the school is located in three rooms, I stayed below a little while to watch a cock fight over which there was much spirited betting, some five or six little boys and girls taking part with their pennies. The native owners of the fighting cocks grinned at me and seemed to think they were giving me a free circus. The fight didn't last very long, one of the birds almost decapitating the other with one stroke of his spur. This steel spur that is placed on the birds is shaped something like a tiger's claw, is several inches long and literally as sharp as a razor, coming to a very delicate point.

After this I went upstairs, giving my cochero orders to wait for me.

I was met at the head of the stairs by a bright-looking native teacher, a young man of, I should say, 25 years of age, smoking a cigarette. After exchanging the usual salutations in Spanish, he invited me to step inside and witness the conduct of the school. I told him I was a newspaper man from Minnesota and he immediately hauled out a railroad map and located Minneapolis. I had great difficulty in getting any information from him or in getting him to put the children through their exercises for me. He insisted on pumping me all the time. He was exceedingly eager for information about the United States. However, he got some little boys to work out examples on the blackboard and to bound the United States for me as well as to read some English from a primer imported from England. There wasn't a single American book in the schoolhouse. The children were all bright, one little fellow who worked an example on the blackboard exceedingly so. He would compare favorably with any boy of his age in the United States, but you ought to have heard the noise in that schoolroom! Pupils left their benches and crowded up around me for the purpose of studying the "macho grande Americano." They raised such a hubbub that the teachers in the other rooms, followed by nearly all their pupils, came in to take a look at the curiosity. The rest of the visit was so much like being in a circus just before the animals are being fed that I was unable to get head or tail to anything that was said to me, particularly as the principal rattled off his Spanish too fast for my ability to translate. I accepted a cigarette and went downstairs amid the yells of about 250 children bidding me "good morning," "good afternoon," "good-bye" and "come again" in English. I found the street deserted when I got down, and being about a mile from the center of the town at nearly 12 o'clock noon, you can imagine how disgusted I was to find my coachman had vamoosed, leaving me to wade through the dust and broiling sun by easy stages to the quartel where I had a good meal with the boys of the Nineteenth Infantry.

  The natives of Cebu are Visayan. They are industrious and as already indicated, quite a number of them in the city have been carefully educated, many of them in the local seminary and several in the universities at Manila.

Politics of the Natives

  There are three daily newspapers in Cebu owned and edited by natives who are above the average natives in intelligence. One of these papers was launched on the sea of journalism during my stay in the city. The editor is a firm believer in William J. Bryan and was anxious to get my opinion as to Dewey's chances against Bryan for the democratic nomination. He said that if Bryan was elected, the Philippines would be allowed to govern themselves. I told him that I thought Bryan would be nominated, but that McKinley was sure of a re-election. This seemed to worry him. He is a born politician. He said that while he had no communication with the insurgents, that he was satisfied in his own mind that the United States would never get control of the Philippines as long as a native lived and could get his hand on a bolo. He discussed the new commission and wanted to know if I thought Judge Taft would report to Washington that the war was over. I told him that in my opinion, Judge Taft would report conditions as they existed, and that he would probably recommend the hanging of all natives who persisted in robbing and killing outposts; that, in other words, he would call such men robbers and murderers and treat them as such. This didn't please him. He acknowledged that the Americans were treating them kindly and justly, but insisted that such a course would not help matters in the least. "Freedom is what we want, and our people will fight thirty years if necessary to secure it," said he. He accused us of bad faith before the outbreak in Manila, and said that he always knew we intended to appropriate the islands. I asked him if he thought the people could get along if they were given their freedom. He said, "No, we would need the protection of a strong power like the United States for a while." I had quite a lengthy discussion with him upon the merits of the Philippine question, and found him to be intelligent, enthusiastic and patriotic. He almost convulsed me with laughter when he said that Bryan would carry the Philippines if his people were given an opportunity to vote next November. I explained to him that the supporters of McKinley in America were claiming the same thing.

-M.J. Dowling

DOWLING DELIGHTS IN MINDANAO'S FERTILE ISLE

Visit to the Fine City of Zamboango—American Troops Fat and Happy—A Few Earthquakes on the Side—A Wonderfully Productive Soil and Climate

Correspondence of The Journal

Zamboanga, P.I., April 21.—This is the chief city of the Island of Mindanao and is 262 miles south and west of Cebu. It was half past 6 o'clock in the morning when we cast anchor in the harbor of Zamboanga. We had been up, however, since 5 o'clock drinking in the beauty of a tropical sunrise. A silvery mist hung over the water and the shadowy outlines of the shore above which we could just distinguish the tall heads of the cocoanut palms. As the sun in a blaze of splendid color dispelled the mist, the tree-lined shore was fully visible—a forest of deep, rich green in the foreground with white houses and brown huts peeping out through the foliage here and there. The houses in the Philippines are all white-washed while the nipa huts are, of course, a sort of somber brown in color.

Zamboanga is situated on the southwestern extremity of the island. The anchorage is open, the harbor being no more nor less than Basilan Strait, the Island of Basilan forming the southern shore of the strait. The tide rushes through this strait at a terrific pace that tests the strength of the native paddler and that of the jolly tar alike. The Strait of Basilan is the highway for all vessels plying between Australia and other south Pacific Islands and the Chinese and Japanese ports, hence Zamboanga does not lack for news from the outside world and many a steamer drops a bundle of papers for the captain of the port. Under Spanish rule, few of these passing steamers stopped at this port on account of excessive charges. They are rapidly changing this order of affairs now and frequently stop for fresh water, vegetables, chickens and eggs. This open anchorage is all that is necessary at Zamboanga, because the typhoon, which is the oriental name for cyclone, does not visit this part of the Philippines; in fact, the typhoon seldom does any damage south of 10 degrees north of the equator. The Island of Mindanao, however, has another elemental disturbance that tends to make one's hair stand on end without notice. I refer to the soul-chilling earthquake. Earthquakes are numerous in Mindanao and it is not uncommon in Zamboanga to have your dishes shaken off your table while you are eating breakfast. Some of the officers stationed here tell me that one gets used to this excepting when the earthquake occurs in the night.

To thoroughly appreciate the location of Zamboango on the Island of Mindanao, it will be necessary for you to examine the map. It is the capitol city of the island and is a case of the tail wagging the dog. The city presents a beautiful view from the deck of an anchored steamer. It skirts the beach and on account of its numerous shade trees has the appearance of being a haven of rest. A pier extends over the shallow water almost as far as deep water, but not quite far enough to permit anything larger than a launch to come alongside. This pier is built of rosewood and the board walk, also of rosewood on it, would probably bring thousands of dollars if transported to some furniture factory in the United States.

Exploring the City

I could not wait for breakfast to commence exploring this inviting city of about 10,000 inhabitants, so I went ashore in the first launch. The main thoroughfare runs parallel with the beach, but it is hidden from it by a row of buildings. The center of this thoroughfare is occupied by what I first thought was an open sewer, but which proved to be an ancient aqueduct that furnishes an ample supply of water from the mountains. It is about four feet deep and ten feet wide through which a shallow stream of clear water flows continuously. The streets are clean and covered with gravel, the buildings are large and substantially built. Our troops are quartered in a vacated convent and are a fine body of men in excellent health, with nothing to do but drill. The natives are all friendly and not a soldier has been killed or wounded out of this command. Adjoining the city on the west is a Moro village composed of nipa huts and governed by Dato Mandi, who lives in a very large nipa and frame combination building where one is surprised to find cane chairs, settees, etc. This dato or prince is a great friend of the Americans. He was born in Zamboango thirty-seven years ago. He desires very much to become a thorough-going American, and in my judgment, has the necessary intelligence. When our troops first landed at Zamboango he was the possessor of three wives and an unknown number of concubines. I visited with him for a couple of hours in his home and he proudly told me that during the past year he has had but one wife and does not intend to have any more. I asked him what he did with the other two whom he had discarded. He informed me that he had sent them home to their parents. He is the father of fourteen children, eight of whom are living. There are six girls and two boys, all of whom are above the average in intelligence and are fully dressed, something quite uncommon among the children of this village. The floors, walls, blinds, stairway and ceiling of this remarkable building are made out of beautiful hardwood, fashioned by Moro carpenters. The prince himself is an easy-going fellow, of quiet demeanor, who is said to be second only to the sultan of Sulu in the power that he wields over the Moros.

This is my first introduction to the Moros, who form the most numerous single race in Mindanao. They are Mohammedans and do not drink any spirituous liquors of any kind, neither do they eat the flesh of hogs. They have many other peculiarities common to the Mohammedan religion. The other inhabitants of this island are East Indians and Visayans, the last named being Catholics. I was very much interested in examining the nipa huts of these Moros to note the difference, if any, from those occupied by the Tagalos and Filipinos. They are, however, very much the same. I loitered around their market place, bought fruit at their little booths, watched the bakers at work and sat down to rest frequently in their little shops. Fruit is ridiculously cheap. I picked up a bunch of bananas numbering seven or eight and threw down a Mexican ten-cent piece for payment. I was astonished to get 9 cents change, making these bananas cost me only one-half cent American. Like elsewhere on the islands, the Chinese have control of the best shops.

Moros Look Like Pirates

The Moros have more of the piratical look than the Filipinos. Their eyes in particular do not tend to make one entirely comfortable in their presence. The female population is ugly beyond compare. I understood that there were slaves among these Moros in this village, but I was unable to discover any semblance of slavery. I was interested in the children, some of whom attend school, but the most of them put in their time playing, very much like the average American children, except that these children are invariably naked and their sports are of a rougher order than those of the children in the United States. I watched a great crowd of them playing at some sort of hide and seek game in the water. They would dive and swim under water, catching one another and then rising to the surface, where they would laugh and chatter away in Malay. Whenever a little fellow was held under longer than he thought proper, he would let out a howl and then cry just as any other injured child would. Generally when one of the little ones cried in this manner, he had someone among the larger children who would take his part and a lively scuffle would follow. On the whole, though, they played with great good nature.

The Fort of the Candles

At the eastern extremity of Zamboanga is the old moss-covered Fort Pilar, where, on Saturday night, one can see a most curious sight. Under the walls of a sealed gate of the fort I saw hundreds of burning candles left there by natives who had spent the evening worshipping the Virgin of Pilar. The story, as told to me, was to the effect that the creek or river used to run through the fort at this point and that a sentinel walking on the wall one night saw the Virgin just outside the gate through which flowed the river. He didn't know who it was and challenged the apparition. It started to walk away, he fired, and the Virgin disappeared in thin air, while the bullet from the soldier's rifle returned and killed him. For this offense committed by the garrison, God caused the river to dry up, and when water next appeared in it, its course was changed so that it reached the sea around the fort. To atone for this offense and to record the miracle, the gate was, by order of the commanding officer, stoned up and sealed and an inscription carved on the pedestal formerly occupied by the stone statue of the Virgin, and now every Saturday night the Visayans pray for hours before this sealed gate and burn innumerable waxen tapers at the foot of the shrine. Great masses of wax or tallow have accumulated, and I am told that the thrifty Chinamen come here when all is quiet and gather this waste material that they may mold it and resell it to the worshippers.

Here is Mateo Francisco

Between the center of the city and the old fort lives Mateo Francisco, the native guide and interpreter who spent fourteen years in the United States in the home of Dr. Steere. This native has been made famous by Dean Worcester. He is a fine taxidermist and has visited most of the islands as a guide and interpreter for several American expeditions in years past. One would think that Mateo would be very much different from the average native, considering the advantages he enjoyed. He talks excellent English. He lives in a nipa hut, the same as any other native, and seems to enjoy the company of domestic animals in the same house in which he lives; in other words, Mateo, like the American Indian, dropped back into his native ways. He is working as a hostler for an American stenographer. One can draw many useful lessons from the career of Mateo Francisco. To thoroughly appreciate his character, one should read Worcester's book on the Philippines.

It is perfectly safe to go anywhere alone and unarmed in the province of Zamboanga. Mr. Russell very kindly furnished me a saddle pony and accompanied me during one whole afternoon and late into the night on a tour of the province. We galloped over excellent turnpikes, having ditches on either side about a foot deep and two feet wide. All the fields were fenced. These fences are made by weaving pieces of bamboo into a sort of mat through which a rabbit could not work its way. Nipa huts are very numerous. All the natives appear to be busy. For miles into the country, we galloped under the shade of towering cocoanut trees, until we came to the foothills of the mountains. We forded a clear stream of pure mountain water and followed bridle paths that took us through deep sand, through vegetation so thick that one could not see a distance of ten feet on either side. We rode over rice fields, through forests of hardwood, and, after making a circle, returned through Tetuan, a native village of some five or six thousand inhabitants. The last few miles we passed hundreds of natives going to their homes from the city. It was late at night. We could not distinguish their features, but they invariably stepped aside, the women bowing and the men taking off their hats and bidding us "good evening" in Spanish. I enjoyed this splendid horseback tour better than any single trip that I have taken in the islands, and I fully agree with the troops stationed here in saying that this is the most beautiful and healthful military post in the Philippines.

The Island of Mindanao

The Island of Mindanao is second in size and for many reasons the best and most important in the archipelago. It contains several ranges of mountains. It has the best and most important rivers, its lakes are so numerous that they have given the island its name, which means man of the lake. It lies in the belt of equatorial currents, its valleys are the most fertile of the archipelago, it is the best situated regarding storms, as there are no typhoons.

Its area is approximately 40,000 square miles. There are about 200,000 Filipinos, an unknown number of savages and about 120,000 Moros on it.

This is the finest island in the archipelago in which to seek the best hardwoods. There are mines of gold, iron, copper, sulfur, mercury, alabaster and coal. Some of the American officers have uncovered a vein of coal so close to the city of Zamboanga so situated as to be easily shipped by waterway in a chute from the mines. Gutta percha is also found on this island. There is a flower said to be three feet in diameter that grows here which gives the island the distinction of having the largest known flower. I saw bats that would measure all the way from two to four feet from tip to tip of the wings. Mount Apo, located here, is the most famous active volcano of the islands and is also the highest peak, being 10,965 feet high. It is situated near Davao. Extinct volcanoes are numerous. The river valleys and the lake regions are enormously productive. From the foregoing, it becomes evident that the most valuable island of the Philippines is Mindanao. Its scenery is varied and beautiful. There is a waterfall not far from Zamboanga that is as beautiful as Minnehaha with the additional attraction of being surrounded by magnificent verdure clad mountains. The volume of water that goes over it is far in excess of that of Minnehaha. The safety with which one may explore this island will undoubtedly bring its many attractions to the notice of our people long before the interior of Luzon and many of the other islands will become familiar to us. Capital may at this time find rich opportunity awaiting it, particularly in the development of the gold and coal deposits and in exporting hardwoods.

  Southerners in the United States will be delighted to learn that Indian corn and sweet potatoes are grown in this island and are eaten with great relish by the natives. Cocoa (chocolate bean) and tobacco are grown quite largely also. In the District of Surigao abaca (hemp) is grown to the value of about 2,000,000 pesos annually. Alcohol is distilled in this district and there are some placer gold mines. In the District of Davao there is a section of about eight square miles where cacao, coffee, palay, abaca, cinnamon, cocoanuts and sweet potatoes are raised in great quantities. In the District of Cottabato, the low plains along the rivers will undoubtedly become the garden spot of the archipelago. It is a district of great fertility. Rice grows luxuriantly, gutta percha is gathered and the coffee grown here competes in Manila with the best brands. This is the best place on the islands for the cultivation of the sugar cane, Indian corn, cocoanuts, tobacco, cotton and cacao. The natives in this district are Moros and a savage tribe called Tirurayes and they are not any too friendly, although as yet but little trouble has been met by the American troops in dealing with them.

In the Island of Basilan, which lies opposite the City of Zamboanga, there is much good timber and the valuable mastic tree is found here in great numbers.

It is with considerable regret that I leave here tonight for the Sulu Archipelago. I envy General Kobbe and his robust men the beauty of their location and the free and easy life they lead. I trust that it will be the good fortune of any Minnesotans who come to the Philippines to have their lines cast in such pleasant places as Zamboanga and surrounding towns proved to me.

-M.J. Dowling

DOWLING PULLS HIS LEG ON THE SULTAN

How His Suluan Majesty's Attention Was Attracted—A Visit to the Beauties of the Harem—City of Sulu and Its Wonderful Charms—Some Wonderful Weapons—The Sultan "Kicks" on the Pay

Correspondence of The Journal

Jolo, P.I., April 23, 1900.—It is pleasant sailing on the Sulu Sea from Zamboanga to Sulu, or as the Spaniards call it, Jolo, and the ninety miles seemed very short. Fish were numerous, dolphins continually played round the bow of the vessel, the spouting of whales was not uncommon, and native boats of all sizes dotted the mirror-like surface giving the tourist the impression that the Moros spend a great deal of time on the water. Talk about your scenery! Here in the Sulu archipelago is where you get it! The Thousand Islands of the St. Lawrence are outclassed, Florida is surpassed, the woods of Maine are not in it, and the Catskills are not more beautiful than these beautiful islands. No one seems to have taken the trouble to count these islands of the Sulu archipelago. There are perhaps seventy-five or a hundred, maybe more. None of them is very large, and the total area cannot be more than 1,000 square miles. Some of the authorities give it about 800. These islands are strung out in a very liberal way from the Island of Basilan southwest to the coast of Borneo. There are no windstorms in this part of the world, and the thermometer lingers around 80 degrees the year around. Every afternoon, somewhere between 12 and 4 o'clock, it rains. There is no mistake about this rain. It comes down in such a business-like way that it leaves no doubt in your mind as to the fact that it is a rainstorm. It simply pours. After the shower, the sun comes out as bright as ever and vegetation, washed by the recent rain, glistens and gleams like a world of emeralds. The earth takes up the rainfall rapidly.

There are fine hardwoods in the forests and bananas grow in great profusion. There were no less than five varieties of bananas offered to us for sale within a half-hour after our ship cast anchor in the crescent-shaped Bay of Jolo. One could get a dozen large, fat, red-skinned bananas for five cents. For the same sum, you could get from one and a half to two dozen of the long, finger-like yellow ones. The best of all, however, are the short, fat, chubby, green-skinned bananas, for which the natives exact ten cents a dozen. The first of these I saw I refused to buy, because I thought they were not ripe. After eating one I refused to buy any other kind. They are the most delicious bananas I have ever eaten. Sugar cane and many kinds of fruit are raised by the natives, and cocoanut trees are numerous. Deer and wild boar abound in the forests. The water buffalo is the favorite domestic animal, cows being scarce and horses seldom seen.

The People of Sulu

The population of the Sulu archipelago is said to be about 100,000. The inhabitants are all, or nearly all, Mohammedans, or, as the Spaniards call them, Moros, and are of the Malay race. They are of a lighter brown color than the Visayans, who are themselves lighter than the Tagalos of the northern islands. The Moros living on the coasts are called Samals, and those in the interior are called Guimbaus. The former hunt, fish and dive for pearls, which are numerous. They are very fierce and warlike, forming in the early days the much-dreaded pirates. The latter devote themselves principally to farming. There is much rivalry between them, which often results in deadly encounters. They make their own weapons. These weapons are the finest in the Philippines. The finest weapon they make is the "kris." I bought a very fine specimen for $12, the blade of which measures two feet, with a bone handle woven with rattan and other strong fibres for a firm hand-hold. A very fancy guard protects the hand, the blade is a two-edged sword with waved edges. The center of the blade is a concave groove decorated with Arabic figures. The steel is superb, and the edge like that of a razor. It is used in making thrusts. Daggers and lances are quite numerous, the former being beautifully decorated and the latter being so nicely adjusted as to be easily thrown with precision, even by a novice. The blow-gun is used, particularly for killing game birds. It is a long piece of bamboo, I should judge about twelve feet long, hollowed out and with a very smooth inside surface. A small arrow, about eight inches long, with steel tip and cotton base is placed inside this gun, which is then raised to the lips and aimed at the bird and with one puff of breath this arrow is sent with unerring precision to the tops of the highest trees. I borrowed one today from a little Moro boy, who was knocking down small birds from the trees in Jolo, and blew on it until my eyes bulged out without being able to get the arrow to go more than two or three feet from the mouth of the gun. By the way, it is the one weapon that I was unable to get a specimen of, because the natives refused to sell them at any price. Bronze cannon are also cast by the natives, who call them lantacas. Spanish is the language spoken in the City of Jolo, though since the advent of the American troops it is correct to say that the English language prevails. Elsewhere in the archipelago, the Malay tongue is used to the exclusion of all other languages. It is a curious thing to know that Malay is not written by the natives. When they write papers of state, etc., they use Arabic. There are only two dialects of the Malay tongue. It seems to be an easy language to learn.

The White City of Jolo

We sailed into the harbor of Jolo at 2 p.m. yesterday. The harbor or bay is almost a perfect half circle with the entrance toward the north. The beautiful white city of Jolo, laid out in perfect squares, at first sight reminds one of the world's fair grounds at Chicago in 1893. All the buildings are white and a high wall enclosing the city is also white. From our anchorage, a most beautiful view presents itself to the eye. Over the white city arose magnificent trees that seemed much greener because of the white surroundings. To the west is the Moro village of Tulai and to the east is another native village composed of nipa huts built on poles extending out into the bay with walks made of split bamboo reaching them. The beach from both villages around the enclosing point of land is covered with native huts. Back of all these arises an amphitheater of hills of considerable height and densely wooded. From the center of the white city extending toward us is a stone pier of considerable length which affords a landing place for launches and small craft. A lighthouse is maintained on this pier. This pier is an extension of the main street of Jolo along both sides of which are splendid public and business buildings of stone and frame, usually two stories high. Rows of magnificent trees form an arch over the street, giving it the appearance of that beautiful elm-shaded avenue in Pittsfield, Mass. The other streets in Jolo are similar to this main street. Beautiful lawns are kept and wonderful flowers fill every nook and corner of the yards. The whole town, which is, as you can imagine, not very large, resembles a well-kept country estate of one of our millionaires in the states. The American troops are under command of Major Sweet and are excellently housed within the walled city. There are two gates to this wall; through one of these the natives are permitted to enter during the day, but before entering, each native is required to leave his arms in a blockhouse about a hundred feet from the entrance. After he has done this, he is permitted to enter and mingle freely with the occupants of the city. A visit to this blockhouse throws a curio hunter into an ecstasy of delight. One can see spears here with gold and silver mountings, tasseled and tufted and most scientifically balanced as to weight. Crisses, barongs, bolos, machetes, daggers and even firearms are hung up in the open space. In the morning hours when the natives come to market, one can see a splendid collection of these arms and this is the best time in which to negotiate with the Moros for the purchase of any of these curiosities. Bolos and crisses range in price from $5 to $150 each. The highest priced ones are inlaid with gold and silver. The scabbards of all are made out of the best hardwood in the islands.

A Visit to the Sultan

This Island of Sulu or Jolo is the largest in the archipelago. It is 97 miles in circumference and has an area of 330 square miles. The mountain scenery is beautiful. The highest peaks are Tamantangis, 2,900 feet, and Babu, 2,700 feet. On the opposite side of the island from Jolo is Maibun, the native capitol and the home of the sultan, who is the religious head as well as the civil governor of the archipelago. I had the great good fortune to meet the sultan and his suite this morning at the home of the Schuck brothers in Tulai. I spent an hour and a half in the midst of the sultan's retinue in a desperate effort to secure a satisfactory interview with his highness. Sergeant Pepper and a private accompanied me to the house and then left me to shift for myself. The house is a large, square frame building, two stories high, with floors of beautiful hardwood. There are a few tables and a number of chairs. The sultan's prime minister was using a chair and one of the round tables in a front room upstairs, busily engaged in writing. He was the most intelligent member of the sultan's household whom I saw. The main room at the head of the stairs was filled with the sultan's body guard, which consisted of about thirty able-bodied Moros, armed to the teeth with bolos, crisses, spears, rifles and shotguns. I did not see a revolver among them. My presence in this room was the signal for an uproar of conversation that for a moment was just a trifle embarrassing. I took off my helmet, wiped the perspiration off my brow and said "good morning" in English and Spanish. No one seemed to understand anything I said to them, and it was in vain that I used all the Spanish at my command in an effort to make myself understood. I was soon the center of what to me seemed an excited group of armed Moros. I was somewhat disgusted at not being able to make any of them understand me and without invitation sat down on a vacant chair to await developments. A Moro woman soon came from an adjoining room and tried to make me understand her Spanish. This woman, I afterwards learned, was the wife of one of the Schuck boys, whom I will refer to again. I managed to make her understand that I was a newspaper correspondent from the United States and wanted to talk with the sultan, whom by this time I discovered to be holding a sort of court in the east room. She managed to inform me that if I would wait a little while she would send for an interpreter.

The Husky Bodyguard

While waiting for the interpreter, I studied the members of the bodyguard, and even felt bold enough to take a peep at the sultan through the open door of his room. The bodyguard is composed of the largest men that I have seen among the Moros. They are splendid types of Moro physique, and each one seems to vie with the others in the splendor of his apparel. They all wear tight-fitting trousers, usually made of silk, a tight-fitting jacket of the same material with a gaudy turban on the head, which usually completes the costumes of each member of the bodyguard. The buttons of the jacket are not more than an inch apart, running from the throat down to the waist, and are either gold, silver or pearl. Buttons are also numerous down the sides of the trousers, but are used simply for ornament. There are no buttons, hooks or any other device placed on the trousers for use, and it was a mystery to me to know how they were kept on until I was privileged to see the sultan dressing himself while he was holding audience with me. I moved my chair so that I could get a good view of the sultan in the next room, and noticed that he was collecting taxes. One of his subordinates would come up the stairs, and after being announced, would be shown into the presence of his royal highness, who sat on a platform raised about six inches above the floor. He sat on his crossed legs, industriously chewing betel nut and expectorating into a cuspidor held by a slave. This cuspidor was made out of half a coconut shell. Another slave stood nearby with a box of betel nut and some sort of green leaves, in which the powder of the nut was wrapped, thus making a nice quid for his excellency.

The juice of this betel nut is blood red, and as it drizzled down the chin of royalty, one is apt to think that his majesty is suffering from a hemorrhage of the lungs.

How the Taxpayer is Milked

The taxpayer, upon reaching the door which leads to the sultan, immediately drops on his knees and face, and remains there until the great ruler squirts a stream of betel juice into the cuspidor, and in a jerky way bids the traveler enter. The taxpayer then moves around to a position directly opposite the sultan and dropping on his knees, places the palms of his hands on the floor and bumps his nose on the floor between his hands three times. He then crawls up to the raised platform and taking the sultan's foot carefully between his hands, raises the great toe until it meets his lips. He kisses this toe as though he had been hunting for it for about twenty years and was filled with joy upon being at last permitted to view a portion of the promised land. If he be a man of importance, his royal highness treats him to a quid of betel nut and without wasting further time, the mathematician and the taxpayer compare accounts, the taxes are paid, a receipt given, and the worthy subject of this most unworthy king bunts his nose on the floor a few times and backs out of the door for all the world like a butler in an old English home. I was surprised to notice that the money used in the payment of taxes in the manner above described was American gold, whose value seems to be thoroughly appreciated by the sultan.

Pulled His Leg on the Sultan

In the meantime, there arrived a tall, full-bearded East Indian, as black as ink, and with smiles as broad as his face. The woman above referred to, introduced him as my interpreter. I asked him if he could understand English, and found him barely able to make himself understood. I told him I wanted to see the sultan and have a talk with him. He said something in Malay to the woman, who walked over to the door and made some kind of a remark to the sultan, who shot two or three killing glances at the interpreter, at her and at me without deigning to make any kind of reply, whereupon I was informed by my interpreter that he was afraid the sultan was too busy. I then tried a maneuver that interested everybody in the building. I took my chair and placed it inside the door of the room occupied by the sultan, and seating myself again, pulled up the leg of my trousers and showed his royal highness as good an artificial leg as ever was made. He quit doing business immediately and looked at me in a surprised sort of way. He said something which I could not understand, of course, and then relapsed into silence. I then pulled up the other leg of my trousers and showed him the mate to the one he had just seen. He spat betel juice furiously for a few minutes and jabbered Malay in great excitement. His bodyguard came rushing in, followed by the prime minister, and I guess every other person in the building. Two rows of these people formed, leaving an open passage between the sultan and me.

    Seeing that I had not created quite enough excitement, I rolled up the left sleeve of my khaki blouse and showed the wondering crowd an artificial arm. This unloosened the sultan's tongue as well as the tongues of the rest of my audience. A perfect Babel ensued. I tapped the three artificial limbs significantly and, taking hold of my head, began to twist it as though I would unscrew it. This was too much for the sultan. He laughed and laughed heartily. He examined the artificial limbs, deigning to come down from his platform to do it. I was as much interested in him as he in me. I was surprised to notice that he was stark naked except for a shawl-like cloth that drooped around him from his shoulders. I sought out my interpreter from the group and endeavored to have converse with the sultan. It was with poor success, however. The sultan got impatient, and desiring to talk with me, sent out for one of the Schuck Brothers.

    While we waited for the sultan's interpreter, his royal highness, without saying "By your leave," began to dress himself. He was assisted by several slaves. He pulled on a pair of trousers that resembled those seen in cartoons of Uncle Sam. His legs went down into them like powder in a horn. The body of the trousers was about twice too big for him and I wondered how he would make them fit. He made two or three sort of pleats in them and with a dexterous twist made the waist fit him. A very beautiful sash was then twisted around his waist several times and tied at the left side, the ends reaching nearly to the floor. He then put on a very fine silk jacket that was not quite long enough to come down to the top of the trousers or the sash. It was buttoned so tightly down the front that a perpendicular line of flesh was visible. A very heavy turban was wound around his head and this completed his outfit except for a sort of shawl which drooped over his left shoulder.

The Official Interpreter

In the meantime, Ed Schuck and two brothers arrived. These Schucks, together with their sister, were born on this island, of German parents. Their father was a sea captain who traded for many years with the natives of this archipelago. I heard some gossip to the effect that he was associated with the natives in piratical enterprises, but could not verify this. Ed is the oldest of the children and was born on the Island of Sulu 31 years ago. He, as well as his brothers and sister, were educated in Germany. They are excellent linguists. The native Moro woman to whom I have referred above, is Ed Schuck's wife and is the mother of two children. She is a relative of the sultan. The Schucks have a thousand-acre coffee plantation six miles from Jolo. They have numerous other interests in the islands. Ed is the official interpreter for the United States garrison. He runs the only saloon in Jolo and lays claim to much valuable property in the city. Upon the arrival of these brothers, I was able to make some headway with the sultan.

I asked him what he thought of the Americans. He said that he liked them very much, that they were a great deal better than the Spaniards. He said that he didn't think the United States Government was paying him enough for their occupancy of the islands and for his friendship.

I asked him how much he was getting, to which he replied $250 a month. I told him that was considered a good thing in the United States, whereupon he called my attention to his large household, giving me to understand that maintenance was quite expensive.

I asked him how many wives and concubines he had. He said he had two wives and thirteen concubines, besides his mother. All of these had to have their servants and with a wave of the hand he called my attention to the thirty men of his bodyguard and his slaves.

I asked him if I might view the harem. He gave me permission and I was taken by two members of his guard to a house nearer the beach, where I had an opportunity to see his female contingent. With the exception of one of the women, they did not give me a very high opinion of the sultan's taste for beauty. The mother-in-law of the group was a very intellectual looking old woman. She, as well as the rest of the women, were decorated with jewelry of great value. The old lady is very vain and to satisfy this vanity in part, she fairly daubs herself with paint and powder. She seemed to be the queen bee of the bunch. Her clothes were much finer than any of the rest and she had more of them.

I was soon satisfied with the harem and returned to the sultan who was preparing to embark on a German ship for the purpose of visiting some of his dependencies. He is short of stature, quite thick set, has some superfluous flesh, his skin is darker than the ordinary Moros, his nose is large and flat, his lips are large, thick and sensuous. He has a low forehead, is broad between the eyes, and has high cheekbones, large sized ears and eyes that scowl at you from under heavy eyebrows. He impressed me as being very lazy, very vindictive and above all, selfishly greedy. His hair is straight and black, very black, and he wears no beard of any kind.

The Old Lady's Trip

In the parade from Schuck's home to Major Sweet's headquarters where the sultan bade farewell to the commanding officer of the American troops before his departure, the sultan's mother was carried astride the neck of an East Indian eunuch. One slave held a large Chinese umbrella about ten feet above the old lady's head, while another slave held a smaller parasol on one side of her in order to protect the delicate brown skin from the penetrating rays of a tropical sun. The sultan and the rest of the suite walked. The different styles of dress, the variety of accoutrements and the lack of order, gave the parade the appearance of an opera bouffe. If some playwright could have seen this parade and the necessary make-up for its production and could place it in some theater of the United States, an American audience would go into hysterical laughter over it. Major Sweet received the sultan to the music of a band and after exchanging salutations, he wished him a pleasant journey and a safe return. The sultan was from 10 o'clock in the forenoon until 2 o'clock in the afternoon coming from Schuck's house to his quarters in the German steamer.

This letter has grown so long that I will mention the sultan's pearls, as well as a number of other things of interest in my next letter.

-M.J. Dowling

NEAT AND MODERN AMERICAN CAMP AT BONGAO

A Rich Pearling Business—Story of the Murder of Four Soldiers and the Revenge Taken by the Men— Dr. de Mey's Magnificent Collections

By M.J. Dowling

Correspondence of The Journal

Bongao, P.I., April 25, 1900.—This island is situated 5 degrees north of the equator in longitude 119 degrees 44 minutes east. It is the most southern possession of the United States. It is the most southern island ceded by Spain to Uncle Sam. There are two islands just to the southward of the one that are still retained by Spain, evidently through an oversight on the part of the American commissioners who negotiated the treaty. The terms of the treaty provide that the United States shall have all the islands belonging to Spain north of 5 degrees of north latitude.

This island is very small; however, it is large enough to contain a very high promontory capped by a sugar loaf rock, which in the days of long ago was used as a lookout by Malay pirates. This sugar loaf mountain is so prominent a feature of the island that it may be seen many leagues away. From Jolo to Bongao, one sails a distance of 110 miles without once losing sight of land. The principal island that one passes on the way is Tawi Tawi, which is separated from Bongao by a narrow strait. By referring to the map, you will notice that Bongao is to Tawi Tawi as Sicily is to Italy. The island is garrisoned by one company of the Twenty-third Infantry, commanded by Captain Cloman.

Wild Rush for Mail

I landed here at high noon yesterday, coming through the heavy sea in the ship's steam launch, the Pennsylvania drawing so much water that she was compelled to anchor three miles out. Several of the light draught ships of our Navy have crossed the bar and entered the fine land-locked harbor of Bongao. We came in under a full head of steam at about the rate of ten miles an hour, tossing right merrily on the waves. Just before crossing the bar, we were met by a sailboat manned by American soldiers, and to our gay toots of greeting from our steam whistle, they replied with hearty yells and a waving of hats. We were the first visitors they had seen in six weeks. We brought mail for them from the United States—mail that was at least two months old, but that was welcome nevertheless. How eagerly the boys crowded around the postmaster! How the magazines and old newspapers were gobbled up! With what an elastic step and beaming countenance the boys walked away with the letters from home in their hands! Some few didn't get letters and disappointment was plainly written on their faces. Those who received a half dozen or more letters were the envied of the camp. We brought supplies of all kinds for the boys, and they were in need of some of them, from what a former Minneapolis man told me. He said they were completely out of shoes and potatoes.

If you can imagine a heavily wooded island with a finger-like point extending to the southward, north of which is the open sea and to the east a fine, land-locked harbor, you will get a pretty good idea of the general outline of Bongao as we saw it yesterday when we steamed around this point to its eastern shore and landed at what must have been once a good stone pier. This pier is now very much dilapidated. It was with considerable difficulty and the assistance of two able-bodied men that I was able to make the landing over the rocks from the launch. Walking up a slight incline to the center of the point of land above described, I found myself in the midst of a number of American soldiers off duty. Several large trees cast a welcome shade and a peculiar stone sentry box with loopholes was close at hand and in a position to guard the landing. Upon inquiry, I found that this had been erected by the Spaniards. After shaking hands with a number of the soldiers, I joined a group of a half dozen and "went up town." You can imagine my surprise when I found that town consisted of a company street, and that instead of glistening white tents one expects to see where troops are camped, we saw a novelty in the shape of soldiers' quarters erected especially for them out of nipa. On both sides of the street were nipa huts, built on numbered lots. Over the door of each hut were the names of the occupants, usually four in number. One of the best pieces of real estate was devoted to a large nipa hut used as a hospital. Another one adjoining it is used as a library and reading room. There were three patients in the hospital, all of whom sat up in their bunks and hailed me as I went in to look around. I stopped to give them a little of the late news and left a couple of magazines with a promise of more when I got back to the Pennsylvania.

The library and reading room did not have to exceed twenty books and perhaps 100 magazines, most of which had been so well used as to have lost all resemblance to their original condition.

Inspecting the Boy's Homes

Major Canby and his clerk, with a chest full of money, came with us to pay the boys two months' salary, and I was very much interested when the bugle call assembled the troops for pay. They appeared and formed in line very quickly and it made one feel proud of his country to see what a magnificent body of men these fellows were. While the men were being paid, I joined a group and inspected one of the nipa huts. I found it absolutely waterproof and decorated with the pictures of the girls that were left behind, with banjoes, violins, mouth organs, rifles and side arms highly polished, pictures of Corbett and Fitzsimmons in the prize ring, gaudily colored pictures cut from magazines and curios picked up around here to be sent or carried home to the States. The cots were no more nor less then steamer bunks arranged on the sides of the huts. The floor is made of sand. The whole interior, as well as the exterior, is scrupulously clean. On a little higher piece of ground, overlooking the balance of the company's quarters, is the headquarters house, a long, low building from end to end. Here I found Captain S.A. Cloman, Surgeon C.F. de Mey and the other officers of the company. These gentlemen were all genial and entertaining. Captain Cloman is the best liked Army officer of any rank whom it was my pleasure to meet in the Philippines. The men of his command worship him. My short acquaintance with him gave me as much pleasure as any one incident on the trip. Dr. de Mey is a French scientist who married an American girl from the blue grass region of Kentucky. He has perhaps one of the keenest intellects in the archipelago. During his leisure hours the past eight months, he has collected and mounted a specimen of every animal, reptile and insect in this and adjoining islands. He has also collected, cleaned, polished, preserved and labeled, in addition to the above, two specimens of every kind of shell that can be secured in these waters. More than that, he has collected the finest specimens of Moro arms that I have seen. In making these splendid collections, the doctor very narrowly escaped drowning twice, to say nothing of his adventures with strange reptiles and insects. He showed me one unknown spider that measures fourteen inches from toe to toe outspread, with his body as large, if not larger, than a full-grown lobster. When the

Pennsylvania sails from Bongao tomorrow, it will carry these fine specimens in several large cases addressed to the Smithsonian Institution in Washington. The whole collection goes as a free gift from the doctor, without seeking notoriety and without hope of reward on his part. This man gets $150 per month from Uncle Sam, while many an upstart, with more shoulderstraps and less brains, with more arrogance and less industry, with more authority and less ability, gets twice, thrice and even more than this.

The Inhabitants of Bongao

Outside of this company of soldiers there are a few Japanese, a few Chinamen and a few natives in the "City of Bongao." The island itself is sparsely settled with Moros who are governed by Dato Tanton and Dato Sakilan. These datos have a sort of partnership control of the natives of Bongao, a large part of Tawi Tawi, as well as the whole of the smaller islands in the immediate vicinity of these. I saw very few natives at Bongao, but I had the good fortune to meet the two datos. They came to call upon Captain Cloman, and brought along with them a coat of mail, which they sold to me. This coat of mail is made of brass rings in the flexible parts attached to pieces of the horn of the water buffalo, fancifully cut. It is tied by a string around the neck and clasped at the breast by solid silver clasps. The breast-plates are all decorated with beaten silver ornaments. Its weight would tend to give one blind staggers in a warm climate. These two datos or princes pay tribute to the Sultan of Sulu. They are very interesting characters. Much to the amusement of Captain Cloman and his subordinates, I exhibited my artificial limbs to the datos. Dato Tanton wanted to know if all of the Americans in the district in which I lived were built like me. He became so interested in me that he exhibited a little savage politeness that is worth mentioning. When I started for the launch with my coat of mail, this dato ordered one of his slaves to relieve me of my load, and accompanied me to the launch to see that the slave placed the armor in the boat, and then stood on the pier and bade me good-bye.

A Pearling Business

Another interesting character that I found in Bongao is Smith Alliston, superintendent of the Philippine Pearling and Trading Company, Limited, of England. Mr. Alliston has spent sixteen years in the tropics and bears a striking resemblance to the explorer Stanley. His wife lives in Manila. Through my glasses from the deck of the Pennsylvania as she lay at anchor off Bongao, I could see seven sailing vessels about the size of a North Atlantic schooner. These schooners form the only pearling fleet in the Philippines. Mr. Alliston is the only white man who has been able to get a concession from the sultan for this purpose. I think he got it through the Schuck Brothers. He denies the payment of any tribute to the sultan. He pays no license to the United States Government. He asks for no protection. Each boat, in addition to the usual outfit of a pearler, carries a complement of rifles and revolvers. Mr. Alliston favored me with some very nice specimens of shells, etc. and gave me much information about pearl fishing, which I have no doubt is quite familiar to my readers. The best pearls secured near Bongao are found in sixty fathoms of water, and to this locality the attention of the lovers of pearls will soon be directed because of the discovery of a beautiful black pearl, which is not numerous enough to warrant the statement that they will ever become numerous or common. Mr. Alliston calls the specimen that he has discovered "the black pearl of Bongao," and prophesies great things for it when once it shall have become known in the capitols of Europe. Of course, every pearl shell does not contain a pearl, but these shells are kept and packed in sawdust and shipped to the manufacturing centers of the world, where they are made into pearl buttons and ornaments. I believe the State of Connecticut buys more pearl shells than any other state or principality in the world. These shells are sold by the pound at the pearling station in the Philippines, where they bring 60 cents Mexican, per pound, including barnacles and sea moss, which form no small item in the matter of weight. Mr. Alliston exhibited a familiarity with the Sultan of Sulu's pearls that betokened a more intimate acquaintance with his royal highness than he professed to have.

The Sultan's Pearls

Right here I will keep good a promise made in my last letter—to describe the pearls of the Sultan of Sulu. The sultan may have lands galore and golden eagles piled high in caves. He may number his slaves by the hundred and his concubines by the baker's dozen, but all these are as nothing compared to the wealth represented in the pearls he owns and admires. According to some written or unwritten law of the Moros, the native pearl fishers must give up to the sultan all the pearls above a certain size, so that the best finds in several centuries are to be found in the possession of this young man. I was privileged to see a small bag full of them while I was in Jolo the other day. The finest specimen was a pearl as large as a bantam egg. It was a perfect sphere with fine luster, for which my friend, Mr. Alliston, has offered the sultan $7,000 and been refused. There is no telling what this pearl would bring in New York. Anyone familiar with the value of pearls knows that the shape and luster are two strong points to be considered. The nearer a pearl comes to being a perfect sphere and the more brilliant its luster, the more valuable it becomes. I saw pearls in the possession of the sultan ranging from the size of a small pea up to the size of one I have just described, and almost perfect in shape and luster. The sultan fondles them like a belle would her jewels, and I am told on the best of authority that when offered what he asks for them, he refuses to part with them unless one is willing to take inferior gems. In passing from the subject of pearls, I cannot understand why some enterprising American capitalists do not furnish Mr. Alliston and his company with a little Yankee competition. Fortunes are being made every month in the pearl fisheries of Bongao. I understand that one small firm in New York City has a small interest in Mr. Alliston's company. This is an opening for American capital in which I would be willing to take a part of the capital stock.

No Saloon and No Ice

There is no saloon in Bongao, neither is there an ice plant. There is, however, a canteen in operation and we took with us on the Pennsylvania beer for this canteen. The men do not drink as much as one would expect, situated, as they are, in the most lonely and far-off post belonging to the United States. Health and sobriety are very noticeable in this little command. Captain Cloman permits the men to take a sailboat and be gone in small squads on a leave of absence of two or three days at a time for the purpose of exploring and hunting. The Moros do not eat the flesh of a hog, hence wild boars are numerous, especially on the Island of Tawi Tawi. Having no ice plant, it is impossible to keep fresh meat at Bongao. Naturally one becomes tired of bacon and dried beef or even canned beef. These small hunting expeditions manage to round up one or two of the wild boars and upon the return of the hunters, the garrison has a feast for one day.

One of these expeditions last January was undertaken by Sergeant Egbert V. De Wolfe, Corporal Leonard J. Mygatt and Privates Webster F. Gibbons, William I. Carter and John A. Greathouse, all of Company H,

Twenty-third Infantry. They had a pass good for seven days. They took a small sailboat, intending to visit a lake on Tawi Tawi and to hunt. A friendly feeling existing between the Moros and the troops, and this not being the first expedition, no thought of danger from the natives was entertained. The first Saturday night out, camp was pitched on Tawi Tawi, three miles from Bilimbing, a large native village. Sunday morning the boys proceeded to this village, arriving at 8 o'clock. They remained there two hours, being entertained in the house of the chief and nicely treated by the natives. The chief himself was absent in Jolo. At 6 o'clock Sunday evening, the natives turned in to help make camp, discover a spring, etc., while four of the men amused themselves by playing whist and Corporal Mygatt, disrobing, went down to the beach to take a bath. No attention was paid to the natives who surrounded the players, and who seemed intent on watching the game. They had no weapons except wood-cutters' tools, consisting of parangs (a sort of bolo used for cutting wood), and native hatchets; but even these were not visible at the time. Corporal Mygatt says that the first things he heard to alarm him were screams and two shots. It seems that a native in the tent sitting behind Sergeant De Wolfe, who, at one time, was a resident of South Dakota, suddenly pulled a parang from behind him and struck the sergeant on the neck, nearly severing the head from the body, killing him instantly. At almost the same time, Private Gibbons was struck on the side of the head and neck, making a hole through the skull five inches long, through which his brain oozed. Private Greathouse was struck on the neck, severing the external carotid artery and exposing the internal carotid artery and spine. Had the parang been a perfect one, his head would have been severed. Private Carter was sitting in such a position as to be protected by the tent, which turned the blow intended for him. Seeing that he was not hurt, another native picked up an oar and struck him with it. As he staggered towards his gun, he was struck with a hatchet, which sunk deep into his spine. Private Gibbons was cut all to pieces and was also shot through the body just below the heart. The natives escaped with four rifles, one revolver and four belts of ammunition. The scrimmage lasted about a minute and consisted of a wild scramble on the part of our men for the guns and a rush on the part of the natives for firearms and escape. De Wolf was killed instantly, Gibbons died within sight of Bongao on the return journey. Greathouse had to hold his head on his shoulders with his hands. Carter was severely injured. The only man in the party uninjured was Corporal Mygatt. Leaving their camp and taking along the body of De Wolfe, the survivors of the party reached their boat on the beach to find that the natives had pulled the plug out and thrown it away. They were thirty miles from home, without means of caring for the wounded and with a heavy sailboat to manage in strong currents. A new plug was fitted to the boat, the dead body of De Wolfe cared for and the plucky Gibbons propped up as comfortably as could be in the bow. Corporal Mygatt and Private Carter took to the oars, while Private Greathouse sat in the stern and actually held his head on with one hand, while he bailed the water out of the bottom of the boat with the other! There were so many muscles on the side of his neck cut that if he let go of his head, it would drop down onto the other shoulder. All of the men displayed those splendid qualities for which the American soldier is noted. They persevered, and finally got within hailing distance of their garrison, when Private Gibbons, the hero of the expedition, died after calling attention to the flag that floated over headquarters. It is said that this plucky little fellow, with a bullet hole through his body, his brain oozing out of a big gash in his head, and his arms and shoulders all chopped to pieces, joked with Greathouse on the return trip about having to hold his head on.

    Naturally, the little garrison was thrown into a state of the wildest excitement upon the arrival of the survivors. The dead were buried and Greathouse and Carter were turned over to Dr. de Mey while Corporal Mygatt accompanied Captain Cloman and forty-five men to the village of Bilimbing. Captain Cloman caused Datos Tanton and Sakilan to accompany him on this expedition, which they did with great willingness. The native population of Bilimbing was wrought up to a high pitch of excitement and expectancy upon the arrival of their princes in the hands of the American troops. Explanations were made and a search instituted for the murderers. They were all found and identified. They were delivered up by the natives with no other excuse than that the men did it to get the firearms, in other words, they killed in order that they might steal. Captain Cloman and his expedition returned with the prisoners to Bongao, where the prisoners were set to work policing the camp. While out some distance from camp early in February, cutting firewood, these prisoners made a dash for liberty. The guard opened fire and the ten prisoners who were responsible for the deaths of De Wolfe and Gibbons were hurriedly sent into their happy hunting grounds. This ended the tragedy of Tawi Tawi, the only one that has occurred among the Moros of the Sulu Islands. Strange to relate, Private Greathouse had his head sewn on his neck and is now doing duty in the City of Jolo, being the only man I ever saw with "his head cut off." His comrades joke him a great deal about it but he gives all the credit to Dr. de Mey and feels so good over his recovery that he has not as yet made application for a pension. The news of the murder and the subsequent killing of the ten murderers has spread all over the Sulu archipelago. The incident has resulted in creating a profound respect on the part of the Moros for the American soldiers and the authority of the United States Government. Enemies of Captain Cloman have endeavored to get him court martialed because of the prisoners being shot. Fortunately, these envious fellow officers of his have not met with good success. There is no reason why they should. If anything irregular occurred, it was not through the command or connivance of Captain Cloman. Regular or irregular, it was one of the best things that could have happened to teach the Moros what Captain Cloman told the sultan when his royal highness demanded $1,000 apiece for the ten murderers who had been shot by our troops. The captain informed him that our government would put in a claim against the sultan for $100,000 for each white man killed, plainly telling him that he considered one white man worth a hundred Moros. Personally, I think he placed the proportion too small.

-M.J. Dowling

THE LIFE OF DR. JOSE RIZEL

Story of the Filipino Patriot—His Murder by the Spaniards—His Memory Reverenced by Native and American Alike

Correspondence of The Journal

Manila, P.I., May 1, 1900.—Perhaps nothing has pleased the Filipinos more than the tendency on the part of Americans to encourage Filipino respect and veneration for the best characters in the history of the Filipino races. Americans have made a distinction between Filipino patriots and Filipino brigands or ladrones. For instance, all Americans take pleasure in paying tribute to the memory of Dr. Jose Rizal. Dr. Rizal is to the Filipinos what Abraham Lincoln is to the Americans. Much has been written about him. It is difficult to separate fact from fiction in dealing with the story of his life. In many respects the story of Rizal is shrouded in as much mystery as that of John Smith and Pocahontas. At any rate, his is a most interesting and ennobling character.

On the second floor of an ordinary Filipino residence at No. 2 Calle Estrande y Calle Jolo, this city, lives Teodora Alonzo, mother of Dr. Jose Rizal. To this point I directed my steps in company with two interpreters for the purpose of learning the truth from the lips of Rizal's aged mother. I found her with a house full of relatives in darkly lighted rooms wherein the tallow dip took one back in imagination to the storybooks of childhood. We were cordially received. I found Mrs. Rizal to be an active, neatly dressed, spectacled woman of 73 years of age. Upon being told the object of my visit, she readily consented to tell me the story of the life of her gifted son. The accompanying picture of Mrs. Rizal was taken especially for The Journal. The picture of Tomas Rizal, the father of the doctor, was drawn especially for The Journal by a Filipino artist, from the only photograph in the possession of Mrs. Rizal. The photograph of Dr. Rizal is the standard copy used by the Filipinos at all services in honor of his memory.

Dr. Rizal was one of nine children, the family consisting of seven daughters and two sons, all of whom survive the doctor. His brother was a general under Aguinaldo at the beginning of the insurrection. He was captured by our forces and paroled. He is living up to the terms of his parole. Nearly all of the daughters reside with the aged mother and one of them in particular is a young woman of considerable intelligence and accomplishments.

Mrs. Rizal answered my questions and told me the story of the doctor's life with evident pride. Among other things she said that the doctor was a firm believer in the eventual downfall of Spanish rule in the Philippines, and that he had often spoken of his great desire to secure the intervention of the United States in behalf of the Filipinos. She said, "If my son had lived, there never would have been an insurrection against the authority of the United States. He believed the American people to be the best governed and the most just nation among all the governments of the world."

Dr. Jose Rizal was born June 19, 1861, in the province of Laguna and the pueblo of Calamba. He was a precocious child. At the age of 2 years and 7 months, he was taught the Spanish alphabet, learning it in three hours. A private instructor was secured for him and his advancement was very rapid, necessitating frequent changes in his instructors, whom he rapidly surpassed in learning. When 11 years of age, he attended the Jesuit school in Manila. His ambition was to go to Europe. He graduated from the Jesuit school with the highest honors. At the age of 14, on the occasion of his graduation, he produced a melodrama entitled "Junto al Pasig," which was received with rapturous enthusiasm by the assembled populace. He won numerous prizes and medals from various associations and became, at this early age, a literary genius whose name was on the tongue of all Tagalos. His poems are often recited in the schools and at the gatherings of Filipinos, and his patriotic stanzas move the people to tears. He studied medicine at the St. Thomas University in Manila, and from there was sent to Madrid, Spain, where he continued his studies in medicine at the Madrid University, where he graduated as doctor of medicine and philosophy. Subsequently, he pursued post-graduate studies in Paris and points in Austria and Germany. It was in the German universities that he got larger visions of the rights of humanity. He was a Roman Catholic, but the socialism of German students taught him to distinguish the practice of the friars from the principles of the church. While in Germany, he wrote a novel in the Spanish language, calling it "Noli me tangere." This novel is really a story of the arrogance, immorality and despotic methods of many of the friars in their relations with the natives. While in France, he published another novel of a political character entitled "El Filibusterismo."

A year or more after the publication of the last of these books, he returned to the Philippines to find that his old mother had been blind for several years. He performed an operation upon her eyes, the description of which leads me to believe that it was the removal of a cataract from each eye. This operation was heralded far and wide, and among the superstitious natives, Rizal became a sort of second Savious of mankind. The blind, the deaf, the dumb and the lame were brought to him in large numbers for treatment. His success seems to have been marvelous. His specialty, by the way, was the eye, ear and throat. The books that he had written while in Europe made no friends for him among the friars and in spite of the fact that the natives flocked to him with their love and confidence, it became necessary for him to return to Europe. After his departure, his relatives were driven from the lands they had rented from religious orders and their property was practically confiscated by the Spanish authorities.

About three years before his execution took place, he settled in Hong Kong where he gathered around him many of his relatives and began the practice of medicine. Pining for Manila, he determined to locate in his native city. Upon arriving at the custom house, papers of a damaging character are said to have been found in his baggage by the Spanish officials. He was arrested and his enemies prosecuted the case against him with vigor. As a result of the trial, he was banished to Dapitan, a small village on the north side of Mindanao. In his exile, many afflicted persons journeyed to him for treatment. Among others was an officer in the British Army whose post was at Hong Kong. This officer had an adopted daughter whose parentage is said to have been German. Her surname is in dispute but her Christian name is known to be Josephine. At any rate, she became enamoured of the doctor and with him formed a pretty romance that has been written about in so many different ways that the truth is hard to find.

In 1896, Rizal was permitted to come to Manila. Unfortunately for him, the insurrection of 1896 broke out in all its fury the very day he landed in Manila, and on Christmas morning, while a parish priest was celebrating mass, some unknown natives murdered him. The next day, Rizal was tried for sedition and rebellion by a court-martial consisting of a lieutenant colonel and eight captains. No particular charges could be proven against him and the logic of his defense counted for naught. He was sentenced to be shot. He refused to see any priests, excepting those from the Jesuit order. The execution took place on the fashionable driveway of Manila—the Luneta—at 7 o'clock in the morning, December 30, 1896, in the presence of an immense crowd and 2,000 regular troops forming a hollow square. He knelt on the curbing facing the bay. A squad of soldiers fired the fatal volley that snuffed out the brightest intellectual light that has shone from out the dense darkness of Filipino ignorance.

Dr. Rizal spoke and read eleven languages outside of the thirteen different Filipino dialects with which he was familiar.

With tears streaming down her cheeks, his gray-haired mother told me these details of the execution. She then led me to a room sacred to the memory of her son. Here I was permitted to look over his instrument cases, both optical and surgical, which I noticed were of French make. She showed me a tray upon which were cigarettes and matches, telling me that these were just as he had left them. And on a little stand in the corner of the room stood a box made out of the beautiful hardwood of the country. It was about 3 feet long, 8 inches high and 18 inches wide. Upon the top board was the following inscription:

....

RESTOS

Del

DR. J. RIZAL

1896

....

This, she said, contains the mortal remains of my son. A single candle burned by the side of this box and the fond mother said, "It shall never go out as long as I live." In this room I was shown clay figures modeled by the deceased. Here were also some excellent drawings and paintings. Copies of his books, unfinished manuscripts and even some of the playthings of childhood were here. No visitor to Manila should go away without paying his respects to Mrs. Rizal.

The romance of the doctor's life consists of his acquaintance with Josephine. One hour before his execution, he and Josephine were married. Some of the halo hanging over this affair was dispersed by the doctor's mother when she said, "That woman married my son in order to get the $2,000 life insurance that he carried." However, that may be the Spaniards drove the widow of the doctor out of Manila after the execution. She lived among the insurrectionists but did not, like Joan of Arc, fight with them. It may be interesting to know, that Josephine is now living on the Island of Panay not far from Iloilo as the wife of another native and the mother of a large family.

    Ponciano, the brother of Dr. Rizal, is living in the town where all the children were born, quietly accepting American supremacy and doing what he can to bring about peace between the Americans and the warring Tagals. When the final history of the Philippines shall have been written, the most stupendous character that will emerge will be that of the martyred patriot—Dr. Jose Rizal.

-M.J. Dowling

PART THREE

The Dowling Report
on
Education in the Philippines

★ Including CONFIDENTIAL Annex ★

– EDUCATION IN THE PHILIPPINES –

Renville, Minn.
July 13th, 1900

To the Secretary of War,
   Sir: –

   When on Feb. 1st, 1900, you appointed me to proceed to the Philippine Islands there to visit public schools established by the military authorities of the United States, I was instructed to report observations and make recommendations, keeping in mind the probable change from military to civil supervision as well as conforming as near as might be possible with the American idea of public education.

   Endeavoring to accomplish this task, I have the honor to report as folows: –

   I arrived in Manila Mch. 14, 1900, and reported to Gen. Otis the following day. Gen Otis very kindly outlined his plans for the education of the Filipinos and directed me to proper sources for information relative to what had been accomplished.

   Gen Hughes organized the first American public schools in the Philippines. At first nothing was accomplished outside of the city of Manila. The first Superintendent of the Manila schools was Rev. Father McKinnon, a Chaplain in a Californian Regiment of Vol. Rev. Father McKinnon was followed by Rev. Geo. P. Anderson, the present Superintendent of Schools for the city of Manila. Mr. Anderson is 35 years of age and un-married. He went to the Philippines as a private in Co. H., 2nd Oregon Vol. He enlisted from Portland, Ore., and at the time of enlistment was a teacher of English language in Portland University. He is a graduate of Whitnam College, Baltimore, and his theological course in preparing for the Congregational ministry was pursued at Yale. His compensation is $2500.00 Mexican per annum and the use of a carometta. He took charge of the Manila schools June 1st, 1899.

   The only additional attempts at supervision of schools in the Philippines are those applied to the Northwest quarter of the island of Luzon where, during the past two months, Capt. J.G. Balance of the 22nd Reg. has acted as Superintendent and in the Island of Mindanao where Gen. W.A. Kobbe has designated a Mr. Russell to act as Superintendent of the schools adjacent to the city of Zamboango. During this time Capt. Balance has established 120 schools in 54 towns detailing soldiers and educated natives to act as teachers.

Outside of manila there have been no attempts at creating a school year, military and climatic conditions naturally interfering with regularity. The schools of Manila were re-opened on Monday, July 3rd, 1899, and closed during the last week of March and the first week of April, 1900. The present school year began on Monday, June 4th, 1900. It is intended that there shall be 9 school months each year. The months of April and May are chosen for the vacation period because of the excessive heat and the prevalence of much sickness among children of school age. During the Christmas holidays there is a vacation of two weeks. All schools are closed on the following legal constituted holidays. (I give the list of last year.)

January 1st,	Circumcision –
January 6th,	Three Kings Day –
February 2nd,	Purification Day –
February 22nd,	Washington's Birthday –
Holy Week	Thursday and Friday –
May 11th,	Ascension Day –
May 30th,	Decoration Day –
June 1st,	Corpus Christi Day –
July 4th,	Independence Day –
August 15th,	Assumption Day –
September 4th,	Labor Day –
November 1st,	All Saints Day –
Last day in November,	Thanksgiving Day –
November 30th,	St. Andrews Day –
December 8th,	La Purissima Conception.

The police of each district in Manila are required to enforce the attendance of all children between the ages of six and 12 years inclusive at some school, either public or parochial. Schools open at 7:30 A.M. and the forenoon session closes at 10:30 A.M. The afternoon session opens at 2:30 P.M. and closes at 5 P.M. The public schools are open every day in the week excepting Thursday and Sunday. Instruction in the English language is compulsory in every public school in Manila one hour each day. The schools for boys and the school for girls are separate, with one exception.

This exception is found at Jolo. In Manila there are 41 public schools in 36 buildings. In the District of Tondo there are two schools for boys and two for girls. In the Dist. Of Binondo there are 6 schools, 3 for boys and 3 for girls. In the district of Santa Cruz there are 4 schools, 2 for boys and 2 for girls. In each of the other districts of the city of Manila there are 2 schools, 1 for boys and 1 for girls. The school for girls in the Dist. of Sampaloc has been recently discontinued.

– MANILA SCHOOL BUILDINGS –

Of the 36 school buildings in Manila, not more than 6 are adapted to the purposes for which they are intended. They are all too small. The 2 best ones are built of brick in a pleasant location but are lacking in playground. The Quiapo school for boys located at Calle Sanpedro #3 is a building constructed by the Spaniards especially for school purposes. It has one large room opening directly on the street where the noise of traffic makes it nearly impossible to hear recitations. Two teachers occupy this room where they hear recitations simultaneously. The light is very poor. One small room back of this answers for a study room. There is not a foot of playground. A cesspool close to the rear entrance of this building emits dreadful odors and the toilet arrangements are something awful. The Sampaloc school for boys at Calle Gastenbide #32 is in a two-story frame building pleasantly situated. Like several other school buildings in Manila, it furnishes a dwelling for the family of one of the teachers. A horse stable is very close to the building and in the same yard. A few shade trees and a number of beautiful plants add materially to the beauty of the grounds which are, in this instance, large enough for a playground. Toilet arrangements are miserable. The Conception School for girls at Marques de Comillas #85 is above the average. The first section school for girls in Binondo at Calle El Cano #33 is reached by going through a narrow alley from a business street up a dark passage way where one is ushered into a dark room in a dilapidated adobe building. The light is poor and the girls have no place in which to play excepting out in the narrow street. The Quiapo School for girls at Villalobos #12 appears to be the private residence of a native lawyer named Ygnacio Ver y Ver. The school is in 3 sections occupying 3 poorly ventilated and quite poorly lighted rooms on the

2nd floor. This school has no playground. The water supply and the toilet arrangements vie with each other in menacing the health of the pupils. The boys' school in Passay has ample playground with no toilet conveniences. This is perhaps the best building for school purposes to be found in Manila province. It is, however, sadly in need of repair. In some of the other schools visited by me, I found the teachers living in one of the second story rooms, while the school occupied the balance of that floor. On the ground floor in these same schoolhouses were to be found stables, open sewers and even hogs and chickens running at large. Some of the buildings are a combination of frame and nipa. Two of them are built of brick and the balance of stone and adobe. Few of these buildings are public property. The rent paid averages about $20.00 gold per month and I was given to understand that the owners deemed themselves insufficiently paid.

– SCHOOL FURNITURE --

I saw no modern school furniture in Manila in the public schools excepting one teacher's desk. The desks for the pupils are old-fashioned forms or benches, the seats being in nearly every instance so high from the floor that the legs of the little ones dangled in the air without support. These benches or forms are long and crowded. If a pupil in the middle of a form desires to come forward for recitation, it is necessary for him to either climb over his fellows or they have to file out to make room for him, either method resulting in much confusion. The teacher's desk looks like a pulpit and is set upon an elevated platform, over which hangs a canopy. In several schoolhouses under the teacher's canopy, where one existed, is to be found a large crucifix. Lithographic charts representing Scriptural scenes adorn the walls, pictures of Christ and the Virgin are not uncommon. Some very antiquated wall maps are seen. Once in a while, a globe is visible. In nearly every schoolhouse, some kind of blackboard space is provided. In some of the schools for girls, prize needlework is exhibited. In one or two instances, I saw primary charts. There is not a single schoolhouse in Manila well equipped with school furniture. The school books were all printed in the Spanish language. Very few primary English books were found in the city with which to equip the English teachers for their difficult task of teaching English without textbooks. This lack of proper textbooks does not occur in the present year however, as a large supply was sent from the United States during the summer vacation.

-- THE TEACHERS --

The majority of the teachers of the Manila public schools are native. This holds good throughout the archipelago. As a rule male teachers are employed in the boys' schools and female teachers in the girls' schools. In the city of Manila there are 23 American teachers employed, 15 of them are females. The American teacher's salary averages $50.00 gold per month. The native teachers are paid about $14.00 Mexican per month which is, I am told, more than they used to receive under the Spanish regime. The American male teachers teach in from 1 to 4 schools, having little circuits. Most of the American teachers have been selected of necessity from the ranks of discharged soldiers and the families of the officers. Some of them have had previous experience in school teaching, others are doing it as a makeshift. Some of them are doing noble and conscientious work. Were I disposed to do so, however, I could find considerable fault with the Americans teaching school in Manila. Two schools are taught by Jesuits, a few by American Catholics. Most of the American teachers, however, are Protestants or are not professors of any faith. I visited nearly all of the schools in Manila and in only one instance did I find a native teacher absent from his post. Nearly all of the native teachers are graduates of the Jesuit Normal School or one of the Universities in Manila. They are intelligent, earnest, enthusiastic and anxious to excel in their work. I met two native male teachers who spoke very fair English. One of them is Ronaldo Caingae who is intensely American and bears the distinction of being the first native to raise and salute the American flag in the Philippines. Right here I desire to state that Old Glory floats in the breeze over every schoolhouse door in Manila during every school day. These flags were presented to the public schools of Manila by Lafayette Post #140 G.A.R. of New York City and were raised with much ceremony on or about Washington's Birthday, 1900.

One school visited by me had an enrollment of 250 pupils and was taught by 1 American and 3 native teachers. This American was a descendant of American parents and was a veritable soldier of fortune. He served as a private in Cuba, Puerto Rico and the Philippines and spent his vacation this year in Australia. His ideas of discipline were evidently brought with him from military life. His boys were punished by being made to stand facing the wall with arms outstretched. In short, this loquacious and jovial youth was a modern Squeers.

The schools in the Quiapo District are examples of what American progress has done for pubic education in Manila. One of these schools – a school for girls – is presided over by Miss Williams, daughter of Capt. Williams of the Third Infantry. She has 3 native assistants. I found her at her post absorbed in her work. She is a born teacher and the sympathy between her and her girls was very apparent. I found 165 girls in attendance. They were neatly dressed, clean and eager. The native teachers taught everything but English reading, penmanship and spelling. The school is divided into 3 departments. Under Miss Williams' direction, the intermediate department sang "My Country 'Tis of Thee" for me. One little girl, Enriqueta Ver, 7 years of age, is a prodigy, reading English fluently and reciting many well-known poems. Her writing would do credit to an American child of 10 years of age.

All three rooms had an air of business about them and the work done by the pupils, especially in English reading, writing and spelling, indicated patient and conscientious instruction. The native teachers, in addition to teaching the "Three R's" in Spanish, Geography, history, etc., taught needlework. There is no religious instruction in this school. Miss Williams told her girls that she prayed directly to God and they seemed to think this proper on her part. She has not disturbed them in the least in their religious beliefs. The other school in Quiapo is a boys' school taught by Mr. John A. Christensen, a Danish American, who had taught 5 years in the United States. His home in the States is Idaho. He is assisted by 2 native teachers. The only English book in the school during the last year was a school primer written by Friar Seimo. With this and his experience as a teacher, Mr. C. has done so well that all the boys of this school can read English fairly well. Mr. C. gets $60.00 gold per month and is worth more. He has not only succeeded in teaching his pupils English but his associates as well. Absolutely no religion is taught in this school. The attendance has not decreased and Mr. C. informed me that the pupils liked to be relieved from religious instruction. The pupils of both the above schools, as well as whose of every other school in Manila, were furnished with a report at the end of the school year last March showing their grade and standing and this they took home to their parents. This report indicates the course of study adopted by the Supt. of Schools for the city of Manila. I give blank report in full as follows:

    Escula Municipal de ------ del distrito de----------
    Clase----------Seccion----------.
                              Manila, P.I. -----------1900
    Sr. D-----------------------

        Muy Sr. mio: tengo el honor de poner en conocimiento de V. las notas que ha obtenido el alumno D. ----------------- en los examenes -------------- curso de 1899 a 1900.

Conducta -------------------	Principes de Geometria-----
Aplicacion -----------------	Geografia Universal-----
English Reading -----------	Geograhpia de Filipinas-----
English Penmanship ------	Historia de Filipinas-----
English Spelling -----------	Principios de Ciencias naturales-----
Lectura en Espanol--------	Caligrafia –
Moral-----------------------	Urbanidad-----
Lengua Castellana---------	Gramatica Castellana-----
Aritmetica -----------------	Faltas de asistencia-----

        (Signed)

                        Principal de la Escuela-

– PUPILS AND PARENTS –

The schools of Manila are crowded with children. One very noticeable feature is the extreme youth of the children. Every school looks like a primary department. Exceptions to this rule are very few. This would seem to indicate that both boys and girls ordinarily leave school at about the age of 12. No matter how indifferent the parents may appear to be regarding the appearance of their children on the public streets or at home, they have evident pride in making them presentable when sending them to school. All the girls are neatly dressed, clean in personal appearance and lady-like in behavior. The boys are better dressed than many of the children of the poorer classes in the large cities of the United States.

A very noticeable feature of the schools is the noise. Under the Spanish system of education, Memory was cultivated almost to the exclusion of Reason. This method of studying aloud is one of the effects of the system. The children are extremely nervous. Anything unusual in or about the schoolhouse throws them into the wildest excitement. They imitate readily, hence they learn to read, write, spell, draw, sing, play musical instruments, etc., without much effort. The boys have no opportunity to play or to work with their hands. The girls are denied an opportunity of playing outdoors but they have a form of recreation in being taught plain and fancy needlework by their teachers.

There is a great deal of sickness among both sexes in school and the attendance from this cause alone is very irregular. Both parents and pupils are very anxious to learn the English language. Some of the parents with whom I discussed school matters, expressed their contempt for the Spanish language and wanted to know why the Americans permitted it to be taught in the schools any longer. Upon being informed that it was evidently done for the benefit of those who were too old to go to school to learn English, they seemed pleased. At the same time, I was informed that the children, upon arriving home from school, took pains to teach their parents all that they had learned during that day, thus creating a sort of University Extension Course. Smoking and gambling are quite prevalent among the boys.

The school population of Manila consists of Tagalos, Chinese, Spaniards, Chino-mestizos and Spanish mestizos. A pleasing feature in the conduct of the schools is the morning salute to the flag. Every pupil, before entering the schoolroom, salutes Old Glory. The teachers are also endeavoring to inculcate love for the United States by having the children memorize patriotic poems. Mr. Jesse George of Kansas is the author of the following lines, which are recited by nearly every boy in the city of Manila who attends school.

"I am a Filipino boy,
And not supposed to know
About the great George Washington
And why folks loved him so.

> But I have heard it said of him
> That from his early youth,
> When accused of naughty deeds,
> He always spoke the truth.
> And I believe that truthful boys
> Will truthful men become
> And be beloved by everyone
> Like the great Washington."

About 5,000 pupils are enrolled in the public schools of the city of Manila. I am unable to state what percentage this is of the school population.

– ISLAND OF PANAY –

I left Manila April 4th on the transport "Pennsylvania", arriving at Iloilo, the principal city on the Island of Panay, the morning of April 6th, traveling a distance of 332 miles. Gen. Hughes is in command here but there is no school. The "Penn." Landed lumber for the construction of a school building. Capt. Mann, the Adjutant General, informed me that as soon as the building could be constructed, the school would be organized. The city, having been destroyed by fire, left no suitable building for school purposes. I visited a boys' school at Molo, two and a half miles from Iloilo The enrollment was 30, the attendance very irregular. This is the only school supported by our military authorities in this vicinity. There are two private schools for girls taught by Spanish women, the parents of the girls paying for their instruction.

– ISLAND OF CEBU –

I was here from April 14th to the 19th inclusive, having traveled 223 miles from Iloilo. Col. McClernand has just assumed command and was paying personal attention to the subject of education. There are no schools on the island outside the city of Cebu, excepting such as may be conducted by the insurgents. About 1/6 of the school population of Cebu is crowded into 5 public schools. The children are being taught by native teachers. Col. McClernand personally visited each of these 5 schools during one of the days

I was in the city. There are no schoolbooks in the English language excepting in one school for boys where I found some half dozen copies of a primer imported from England. There are 150 boys in attendance at this school. The principal was a bright young native who thought nothing of smoking cigarette after cigarette while conducting recitations. A very noticeable feature of these schools in Cebu is the superior ability of the boys and girls to master mathematics. In the Manila schools I found very few children capable of understanding the simplest mathematical problems. The children of Cebu, however, are not very well advanced in English which is probably due to their having no American teachers. The schoolhouses here compare favorable with those in Manila, they are neither better nor worst. The school population consists of Visayans mainly. They have better physique than the Tagalos of Manila. A very intelligent class of natives administer civil affairs in this city and are exceedingly anxious to have more schoolhouses equipped with American teachers and furniture, for which they expressed a willingness to tax themselves. The Catholic religion is being taught in these schools although one of the teachers expressed himself in no uncertain terms against the friars and their methods. The children generally in this city wear little or no clothing. This is true of both sexes. Those attending school, however, are fairly well dressed.

– ISLAND OF MINDANAO –

I traveled 262 miles from Cebu to Zamboanga where there are 2 excellent schools, 1 for boys and 1 for girls. The school for boys is in a building especially built for school purposes and outside of sanitary arrangements is well adapted to this purpose. The boys have plenty of playground and use it. The girls are taught in the church building. Native teachers only are employed. There are no schoolbooks in the English language. Every town in this province has 2 schools, one for each sex. The school building at Tetuan is especially worthy of notice. Under Gen. Kobbe, Mr. Russell, who has charge of the public schools, has built, with native assistance, the best schoolhouse in the Philippines. Sanitary arrangements are excellent, the grounds have been cleared of brush and trees, plants have been set out and climbing vines have been trained over the building. Altogether it has a homelike and attractive appearance. The natives appreciate what has been done for them here and in the course of a horseback ride with Mr. Russell through the outlying districts of Zamboanga, I was pleased to notice that all the natives called Mr. R. by name and doffed their hats to him. The school population in Zamboanga and surrounding districts is composed of Moros and Visayans. The Visayan children are more intelligent than the Moros. As great progress has been made here in schoolwork as has been accomplished in Manila except as to the teaching of the English language. The supervision of the schools is excellent. The attendance is good and the health of the children notable.

– ISLAND OF JOLO –

I reached the city of Jolo after sailing 90 miles from Zamboanga on Monday, April 23rd and visited the only American school in the Sulu Archipelago. It is conducted by an intelligent East Indian teacher inside the walled city of Jolo in a basement room of a building close to the commanding officer's headquarters. The teacher was imported from Borneo and is an excellent scholar in the English, Malay, Arabic and Spanish languages. His salary is $80.00 Mexican per month. His pupils number less than 50 and among them are Filipinos, Moros, Mestizos, Chinese and Spanish of both sexes. I do not hesitate to say that this is the best little school so far as results are concerned that I have visited in the Philippines. The pupils all read and write excellent English and recite intelligently in Geography and Mathematics. A few more teachers like this East Indian could be profitably employed among the Moros. The schoolroom, with its damp, earthen floor occupied by this little body of children, is responsible for an unusual number of colds which prevailed among them at the time of my visit. This is remarkable when one considers that colds, catarrhs and kindred troubles are almost unknown in the Philippines. Our commanding officer at Jolo, Maj. Sweet, is constructing a large, two-story frame building outside of the walled city and near the Moro village of Tulai. An architect from Manila was superintending its construction at the time of my visit. He had the frame up and stated that in 6 weeks the building would be ready for occupancy. This school will, of course, be filled with Moro children to the exclusion of others.

– ISLAND OF BONGAO –

I arrived here at 12 o'clock noon April 24th, distant 110 miles from Jolo. It is a beautiful island with an excellent harbor and is garrisoned by one company of the 23rd Infantry in command of Capt. Cloman. I found no school established here and saw but few children although there are two Datos or Princes here which would indicate a large population. Our troops are nicely housed in nipa huts of their own construction together with hospital, library, etc. It would be an easy matter to construct suitable schoolhouses and I have no doubt but that the men would enjoy being detailed for duty as teachers. Dr. Demey, the contract surgeon, is an excellent scholar in the Malayan tongue and would be of great assistance in establishing a school. This island is in Lat. 5 degrees North and Longitude 110 44 E. From this point I returned to Manila, stopping at Jolo and Iloilo. I arrived in Manila the evening of April 29th and sailed for the United States May 5th on the Transport "Meade."

– HIGHER EDUCATION –

In order to understand the educational system in the Philippines it is necessary that one should know something of the schools for secondary education, Normal Schools, Universities, School of Arts and Trades, School of Agriculture, Nautical School, School of Painting and Sculpture and Theological seminaries. For information relative to these, I would respectfully refer you to the report of the Philippine Commission to the President of January 31st, 1900, Vol. I, Pages 35-40 inclusive. This will confine my observations and conclusions to the common or public schools.

– CONCLUSIONS AND RECOMMENDATIONS –

My observations have convinced me that the natives of the Philippines are capable of and eager for advancement. Public education in the islands previous to American occupation, gave them but little opportunity to exhibit their capability. The city of Manila particularly offers a fertile field for transplanting the best that we possess in the way of a model system when it shall have proven its worth and adaptability. The expense of establishing this system will be considerable. The annual appropriations for maintenance would not need to be burdensome and can be levied as a local tax without meeting any objection from the residents either native or foreign.

I would recommend the immediate purchase of at least one tract of land for school purposes in each of the districts of the city of Manila. This tract should be not less than 300x300 feet and centrally located. A suitable building should be erected in the center of each district and, that the customs of the people may not be ignored, the sexes should be taught in different sections of the building. I would make these buildings models especially as to sanitary arrangements. I would beautify the grounds and place suitable furniture in each room and thoroughly equip every school. For at least 2 years I would place an experienced American teacher in charge of each one of these schools. I would urge a very careful selection of teachers for this purpose. Their compensation should be very liberal. I would urge the appointment of English speaking native teachers to the best positions. In the beginning, I would make the compensation for these teachers who can read and write the English language intelligently noticeably higher than that received by their less progressive associates. I would establish temporarily a normal school for the instruction of natives now holding teachers' certificates, graduates to have preference for appointment in the public schools. In this school, I would teach the English language and the history, geography and civil government of the United States. This instruction should be free and I think it would be good public policy to go a step further and pay the living expenses of those in attendance, making the course from 3-6 months and requiring from each one in attendance a contract to teach in the public schools of the Philippines at least two years.

I would make attendance on the part of pupils in the public schools rigidly compulsory. I would place the teaching of the English language first in importance and make the teachers the best paid of the government employees. Conditions in the Philippine Islands at the present time are such that stenographers, interpreters and even copyists are much better paid than the teachers in the public schools. A competent physician should periodically make a careful examination of all the children in each school for the purpose of rooting out dangerous, contagious and infectious diseases. It is unnecessary to suggest that advisability of placing at the head of this system as capable and experienced a man as can be induced to leave his position as city superintendent of one of the larger cities of the United States. I would recommend the appointment of one good American teacher under contract for 2 years to the position of city superintendent in each of the larger towns outside of Manila. He could teach the native teachers as well as devote an hour each day to every school for the purpose of spreading the English language. His authority might be extended to cover outlying districts and he would then have the nucleus around, which would grow a system that might in time rival that to be established in Manila.

In the outlying districts where nothing but military authority exists, I would recommend the continuation of the present system of establishing free public schools and appointing native teachers and detailing private soldiers to act as teachers of the English language. If the course above outlined were adopted, the General Superintendent or Commissioner of Education for the Philippine Islands would be in close touch with all of the schools in the islands and as rapidly as conditions would warrant, he could appoint a Superintendent for each island, who would have general supervision of all the schools on the island and could devote all of his time to visiting and supervising them.

I would especially recommend the establishment of manual training schools. In my judgment, the manual training school is next in importance to the free public school. I see no necessity for the expenditure of large sums of money for the establishment and maintenance of colleges, universities, etc., in the Philippines at the present time. There are enough schools established for higher education to meet the needs of this population for many years to come. The establishment and proper equipment of the public schools will be very expensive but, in my judgment, not so expensive as not to warrant the establishment of at least one manual training school for the boys in Manila, in Iloilo and in Cebu.

Public funds may be properly expended in the maintenance of schools for agriculture, the nautical school and for the establishment and maintenance of manual training schools and at least one military school.

The Filipino people are eager for education and will welcome with open arms the establishment of the American secular public schools. Some little objection may be raised by the priesthood to the omission of religious instruction. The American idea of a free conscience, free speech and free press will undoubtedly prevail, however.

        Respectfully submitted,
        -M.J. Dowling

– CONFIDENTIAL REPORT TO THE SECRETARY OF WAR –

Education in the Philippines

Renville, Minnesota
July 13th, 1900

To the Secretary of War,

Sir: –

Having been appointed by you February 1st, 1900 to examine into the condition of public education in the Philippine Islands, I have the honor to submit the following confidential report in addition to the report covering my observation and investigations.

I reached Manila March 14th and remained in that city three weeks. On April 4th, I sailed on the U.S.A. Transport "Pennsylvania" and visited the schools at Molo on the Island of Panay, Cebu on the Island of Cebu, Zamboango and surrounding districts on the Island of Mindanao and Jolo on the Island of Jolo or Sulu. I also landed at Iloilo and Bongao but found no schools established at either point.

I covered 1759 miles, traveling on water in visiting the above points and returned to Manila the evening of April 30th. I sailed from Manila on the U.S.A. Transport "Meade" May 5th.

While I was in Manila, General Otis appointed Captain Todd Superintendent of Schools for the archipelago. I had suggested to General Otis the evident necessity for general supervision over the schools of all the islands but I think the incumbent of such a position should be especially trained in educational matters.

From Catholic sources I learned that in 1897 there were 2167 public schools in the archipelago and that this number did not include universities, colleges, normal schools and convents. I was unable to learn from any source whatsoever the number of schools in operation under American control.

I found Rev. George P. Anderson in charge of the city schools of Manila. He is a Congregational Minister, 35 years of age and was a private in Co. H. of the 2nd Oregon Volunteers. He has had very little experience in public school work and so far as I was able to learn has had no experience as a Superintendent of city schools. He is paid $1250.00 gold per annum. His assistant, Mr. Jesse George of Kansas, impressed me as a capable man for the position. From all I was able to gather relative to Mr. Anderson, I would recommend that he be given an opportunity to resign. I do not believe that he has the ability, the diplomacy and the judgment needed in the position he occupies, particularly on account of his well known prejudice against the Catholic religion. My judgment is that it would be well to appoint someone from the United States who has had experience in the management of city schools and who is not a preacher of any denomination. I believe that such a man can be found provided the salary of the position is raised to at least $3,000.00 gold per annum.

The 36 buildings in which the 41 public schools of Manila are housed do not answer the purpose for which they were intended. In addition to being too small, they lack the most common sanitary conveniences to such an extent as to endanger the health of every child in attendance. Very few of these buildings are public property. I would recommend that suitable sites for public school buildings be secured while it is possible to do so without paying exorbitant prices for real estate.

The furniture of these school rooms include old-fashioned forms with seats much too high for the children and an elevated platform with a canopy under which there is usually a large crucifix. The walls are covered with lithographic charts representing Scriptural scenes. The whole interior looks more like that of a Catholic parochial school than of an American public school. All the native teachers are Catholic, who devote a part of their time to religious instruction. A tactful city superintendent could cause the removal of all these evidences of a parochial school by re-placing the forms with suitable desks and the charts, canopies, crucifixes, etc. with modern wall maps and pictures such as are usually found in the common schools of the United States. If a complete change in each schoolroom was made, it could not be said that the religious sentiment of the people, the priests and the teachers was not respected, as might be said were the religious emblems alone removed.

The present force of American teachers in Manila is not a representative one. It consists of men and women who happen to be available. A few of them have had previous experience in teaching. Some of them are discharged soldiers, some are daughters of Army officers, a few are adventurers. Most of them are teaching for what money there is in it and only as a temporary occupation. In most of the schools that I visited in the city of

Manila, I found the American teachers absent and in several instances learned that they were engaged in other profitable enterprises. The native teachers, with only one exception, were at their posts.

I would call your attention to the fact that there are two or three public schools in the city of Manila in close proximity to licensed houses of ill-fame. One of these schools is a school for girls. I would urge, in connection with this, that licenses for places of this character and for saloons provide for their establishment and maintenance at a distance of not less than 300 feet from any institution of learning.

In recommending that teachers from the United States be employed under contract to serve two years in the Philippines in my regular report to you, I desire to add thereto that I believe male teachers only should be employed. They can stand the climate much better than American females, need less protection and are less liable to become the targets of current gossip. I believe that 15 well selected male teachers from the United States could be placed on a school circuit in the city of Manila so that each could devote an hour a day to 5 schools for the purpose of teaching the English language.

Philippine children are as quick at taking new impressions as are American children and these teachers should be selected with great care so that they may be examples to the children and their parents of what Americans are as a class – strong physically, morally and intellectually.

The present American colony in Manila does not reflect the American high ideal of virtuous womanhood. From what I observed and learned relative to the female nurses in the Army hospitals of Manila, I cannot advocate too strongly the absolute exclusion of women from all government positions in the Philippine Islands until such a time as Americans stationed there shall surround themselves with their families and home influences. The work of educating the Filipinos both in and out of school will necessarily be accomplished as much by force of example as by percept.

I will not occupy your time by relating discouraging details that can be promptly and effectively corrected by competent superintendents in the various islands. I think that native teachers should be taught the English language as soon as possible and that the use of Spanish in the public schools be rapidly and effectively reduced to the minimum as a means of instilling knowledge.

In closing this report I cannot but express admiration for the great work done by your representatives in the Philippines in the matter of education. They have met and overcome difficulties unknown in America and, in spite of discouraging circumstances, have made real progress in the work of educating the Filipinos. Much remains to be done but what has been accomplished gives great promise for the future.

I desire to especially commend the good work that is being done on the Island of Mindanao. Gen. Kobbe is paying particular attention to education with excellent results. The only school on the islands where male and female pupils occupy the same room and are taught by the same teacher is at Jolo. This school is taught by an East Indian. The pupils read, write and speak English better than those of any school I visited.

I cannot close this report without referring to Father Doyle and his associates in the Jesuit College at Manila. I believe that this institution could be fostered by our government through its value as a distributing point for marine information. If a thorough American Jesuit of fine mental attainment and patriotic impulses could be given a chair in this college for the teaching of the English language and the American history and geography, the effect of his work would stamp itself on the character of the graduates of the institution. It would, in my judgment, be the "acorn from which great oaks would grow." I would suggest that this result might be brought about through the aid of Archbishop Ireland of St. Paul or Hon. Richard Kerens of Missouri.

The religious sentiment of the people is very strong and the less attention paid to that branch of education by our representatives, the better. The various religious sects will endeavor to furnish teachers for our public schools in the Philippines and the Catholics will view with suspicion any act tending toward encroachment on their present complete control. If Americans in authority will simply teach secular knowledge without endeavoring to instruct native teachers as to their method of teaching, thereby totally ignoring the religious question, I believe religious instruction will gradually be eliminated from the schools. Any effort to drive it out will tend only to make it flourish.

A great aid to education in the Philippines would be the organization of an excursion, consisting of one bright capable native teacher from each island now occupied by us outside of Luzon and say a half dozen teachers from the city of Manila to the United States where they could visit some of our leading schools and the city of Washington with all its government buildings, etc. This excursion should be in charge of a competent guide and accommodations and entertainment should be first-class in every respect. The expense to the government would be slight when compared with the results that would follow.

If this excursion could be landed at San Francisco January 1st, 1901, the teachers would have an opportunity to see our schools at a time of year when they are in best working condition. This idea was suggested to me on account of the number of natives, male teachers, who expressed a desire to have an opportunity of seeing the United States. Since my return, I have noticed the application of this idea to the islands of Cuba and Puerto Rico.

To summarize, I would say – Emphasize the teaching of English, ignore religion, establish manual training schools and a temporary normal school, select a corps of first-class American teachers, pay them well and build model schools in Manila thereby creating a standard for emulation.

                            Respectfully submitted,
                            -M.J. Dowling

APPENDIX

THANK GOD, I AM NOT A CRIPPLE

AN INTIMATE STORY OF MICHAEL J. DOWLING

BY THE ONE WHO KNEW HIM BEST

MRS. MICHAEL J. DOWLING

Across the front of one of the finest schools in Minneapolis, is written the name "Michael J. Dowling," and it is the story of that man I am going to tell you–that man, who, in spite of the fact that he had neither hands nor legs, made his life an eminent success and an inspiration for thousands of children and men and women. The stimulating story of Michael Dowling's life belongs not only to the school, not only to Olivia, the town in which he lived, but to all of Minnesota–even to the whole country. No man or woman who has heard this remarkable man's story can fail to feel an uplifting of his own outlook on life, and a slight tug at that inner consciousness that served as a barometer for our failures and successes.

Michael Dowling was just fourteen years old when he set out in the back of a lumber wagon to say goodbye to his pony. The youngster, born in 1866, had lived in Huntington, Massachusetts, until his mother's death when he was ten years old. Then he went with his father to St. Louis and later to Chicago. A little schooling here and there–that was all he had. When he had finished a successful summer in Minnesota herding cattle he decided that he needed and wanted more education, so he prepared to spend the winter in town. But his beloved pony! He must say goodbye to him. So this fourteen year old boy–who knew Minnesota blizzards well, was accustomed to them, and had brought his herd of cattle through more than one that had daunted hardier cowboys than he–this boy started out to say goodbye to his pony, and came back to Canby with frozen legs and hands.

The day was clear and cold, but before the two men and the small boy in the back of the wagon had gone far, a blizzard, such as only Minnesota knows, swept up across the prairie. There were no markings, no fences, nothing, and when the stinging snow came faster and faster the two men whipped their horses into a frenzy. The sooner they could get to shelter, the better for men and horses! The lumber wagon careened unsteadily over the wind blown prairie, rocking to and fro, the horses galloping blindly, the men yelling and whipping the horses. They were bent for shelter. The noise of the wind, the wagon, and the wild snow blowing and whistling all about them, left little chance for even the husky voice of a boy to be heard. But there was a voice. The wagon had struck a furrow of plowed ground, and Michael had fallen out of the wagon.

He was stunned at first, but when he jumped up and heard the wagon tearing off in the distance, he yelled as loudly as he could. But they did not hear him, and he was left there alone with only the howling storm for company. He ran after the wagon, but could not catch it. Soon, he was unable to find the track of the wheels. He tried to find the railroad, but it was not where he had figured it to be, for in the wild chase of those two horses, the trail had been lost completely. But this strong, young man kept going, hoping to find a farmhouse. He was tired, and blinded by the snow, but perhaps there was a chance.–Then he struck a woodpile. That meant a farm house, surely. He climbed to the top of the pile and threw sticks in every direction, just as far as he could. He listened for the sound which he expected when a stick would hit the side of a house, but none came. Then he climbed down, took an armful of sticks, and walked fifty feet from the woodpile in every direction, and threw sticks. The result of this, in spite of his careful calculations, was that he lost the woodpile.

He wandered around for a long time, and finally stumbled upon a straw pile. He got into the pile and covered himself with the straw. He was warm now, and slightly sleepy. Well he knew the danger lurking in that sleepiness, however, and he fought against it. Tucked in the straw as he was, it was impossible for him to do more than fight against sleep, and that he did. When he finally crept out of the straw pile, he saw a great red sun peeping at him. The storm was over. Then the boy saw a farm house not more than half a mile away. He was overjoyed and jumped to his feet with the intention of running to the farm house. But he could not stand. He fell down, got up, fell down again. Finally he was able to keep his balance and walked on two rigid stilts to the farm house. His hands were stiff and white. Close to the farm house he saw one of his sticks of wood–it had missed the door of the house by two feet. Michael knocked at the door, and the farmer's wife opened it.

He knew her, and she knew him well, but Michael saw her look at him with amazement. He found that one side of his face was frozen stiff, while the other was perfectly natural.

The farmer's wife and her family got the boy into a tub of ice cold water and started to thaw him out. That was misery true enough. A doctor came and massaged Michael's legs and hands, but he did not believe that the boy would live. Nevertheless, he did his work so well that Michael never after had any complications. The two legs were amputated six inches below the knees, the left arm below the elbow and the fingers and part of the thumb of the right hand. Hard? Michael thought for awhile that death would have been easier than all this pain, with only a life of helplessness to look forward to. But that very idea was one which finally gave him the strength he needed. He was robust, had always led a healthy life, and was surviving the operation well. And now when he heard the neighbors pity the "poor boy who is an invalid for life," something in him rose up and said, "I'll NOT be an invalid, a helpless dependent all my life!"

He sold his cattle and his pony–that beloved pony– and lived for a short time on the county. He had to. But finally he told the commissioners that if they would give him two terms at Carleton College, he would never be a burden for them again. The men perhaps thought that the idea was absurd, but they agreed and Michael went to Carleton College for one year. He had artificial limbs to begin with and the finest kind of courage, so that when he came out, he was fit for life. He taught country school, and in the summer did odd jobs–successfully. Then he was principal of the school at Granite Falls, later superintendent of schools at Renville.

Later, Mr. Dowling became president of the Olivia State Bank, speaker of the House of Representatives, president of the Yellowstone Trail Association, of the Minnesota Bankers' Association. He drove his own car as a matter of course, walked a great deal, was active in every kind of thing that presented itself. He was married and had a family of three daughters.

If you walked down the street and met a large man with a strong, intelligent face and a beaming smile, a man who bent his knees a trifle awkwardly but not noticeably so, a man with a firm handshake, a determined but kindly voice, an authoritative manner–would you say that you had met a cripple? Hardly; you met a MAN among men. Mr. Dowling was the last man to deny that he was physically lacking certain members, but he was the first to deny that he was HANDICAPPED!

"Thank God I am not a cripple!" Michael Dowling often said with a ring in his voice, and he meant every word he said. "A man may be worth a hundred thousand a year from his neck up, and not a dollar a week from his neck down!"

Being crippled, in Mr. Dowling's mind, was having a dwarfed and crippled mind, even while its owner possessed a healthy body. The fun and the glory of danger and achievement are known only to those who have something to struggle against and who come out smiling.

Soldiers, naturally, have a struggle, and in the recent war it was difficult for many of them to come out smiling. Mr. Dowling had experiences enough to have the vision of their outlook upon life if they came through handicapped for life. He realized that the country was going to be unprepared to give them the necessary good cheer and backing that they would need to take hold of life again and make it worth their while. He could feel that first sinking sensation they would have when the war was over, and they, without hand, foot, or eye, would have to find something else to struggle for.

So this splendid man, with his Irish wit and inspired purpose, went from hospital to hospital, a living example of what a wounded and crippled man could accomplish with only a body, a head, and part of one arm.

At a great meeting at the Hippodrome, in New York, arranged by the Red Cross for disabled soldiers, Michael Dowling spoke with such eloquence and power that ex-Governor Charles E. Hughes, who presided, said he had never heard a more powerful speech. After this he was filmed by the government, and his smiling face become familiar to many disheartened soldiers.

Michael Dowling's fame reached other shores. He was invited by the British Ministry of Pensions to visit England, and speak to the disabled Tommies, and there he was received by the king and queen. What his service of inspiration to wounded soldiers has been can never be measured, but his spirit goes marching along on other artificial legs.

So, in spite of the fact that he had endeavored to be of more active service to his country during the World War, Michael Dowling found that his personality fought battles for his country in the cheering of its weary returning soldiers.

Michael Dowling died in 1921, after devoting most of his time and energy to spreading good cheer and a new spirit of hopefulness among thousands of disabled men. Although always a fighter, the exertions of his lecture tours told on him, but he would not quit until over-exertion took his life.

Michael Dowling's memory after death seemed even greater than his fame at any time in his career, for out of public regard for him came two well-known institutions, the Minneapolis School of Crippled Children and the State Hospital for Crippled Children in St. Paul. Not only these honors were made a tribute to him, but a Dowling "Courage" medal was also issued in his memory.

With the assistance of the Rotary Club, a school for crippled children had been carried on in an old church, and busses provided to transport the forty or so crippled children from home to school, and home again.

Headed by Mr. Dowling, the Rotarians succeeded in having a bill passed by the state legislature in 1921 providing state aid for the education of crippled children of the state to the extent of two hundred fifty dollars a year for each child. In the fall of 1924, the unit, having outgrown its original quarters, moved to its present location, a new one-story brick building built especially to meet the needs of the crippled child. The site for this new building, a wooded lot of twenty-one acres on the west bank of the Mississippi River, was given to the city for this purpose by the late Mr. Wm. Henry Eustis, philanthropist, who was also a cripple.

It is fitting that Michael Dowling's memorial is not carved in stone and bronze–that the $100,000 raised by the State and citizens to express their faith and love for him did not go into a towering shaft. Rather, it was put into a school where crippled, handicapped children might find the inspiration Michael Dowling had given them.

The Dowling School for Crippled Children stands a living tribute to Michael Dowling, the man who visioned the needs of crippled children.

Bibliography

Minnesota Historical Society, St. Paul, Minnesota
    Dowling, Michael J. and Jennie B. Papers 1883-1944. Microfilm rolls 1 and 2. Portions copyright by Dowling Family.

    Faries, John Culbert. A Biography of Michael J. Dowling. Unpublished manuscript received from Henrietta "Hattie" Bordewich.

Newspapers

New York Times 1900-1902

Minneapolis Journal 1900

Renville (MN) Star-Farmer 1900

Olivia (MN) Times 1900

Books

Linn, Brian McAllister, *The Philippine War 1899-1902*, University Press of Kansas, 2000.

Fulton, Robert A., *Moroland 1899-1906,* America's First Attempt to Transform an Islamic Society. Tumalo Creek Press, Bend, Oregon 2007.

Ellis, Edward S., *The Life Story of Admiral Dewey,* A Complete History of the Philippines and Our War with Aguinaldo. W.E. Scull 1899.

Lehmann, L.R., *Blizzard* (Paperback), Quik Read Press, Salt Lake City, 1997.

Bottge, Adrian. *Adrian Looks Back.* Renville, MN. Renville Star-Farmer and the Historic Renville Preservation Committee. 1988.

Articles

McClernand, Colonel E.J., *In the Philippines,* New York Times, May 24, 1900, Page 6.

Olsen, Prudence Tasker, *As I Knew Dowling.* Minneapolis Journal September 10, 1921.

Dowling, Michael J., *A story of rehabilitation by a cripple who is not a cripple.* Annuls of the American Academy of Political and Social Science. November 1918: 43-50.

Brown, Gary, *The Sultan of Sulu, The Repository.* (Canton, Ohio) July 13, 2009, Page A-2

Other

Prichard, Dorothy Dowling., *Memories.* (Typed, spiral bound). 1980. Also, personal conversations and copies of letters from her father. Various dates.

Mullett, Mary B., *Dowling Just Wouldn't Give Up. A Wonder Story of Pure Grit.* American Magazine. (Reprinted by Renville County Dowling for Governor Club) Pamphlet. 1920.

Jepson Brothers (Winkley Artificial Limb Co.) *A True Story of a Self Made Man,* Hon. Michael J. Dowling. Pamphlet with Photographs. 1902.

Dowling, Mrs. Michael J., *Thank God I am Not a Cripple.* An intimate story of Michael J. Dowling by the one who knew him best. Pamphlet 1924.

Rubin, Joseph N., *History, The Sultan of Sulu.* Canton Comic Opera Co., Theater Program, Canton Ohio, July 2009.